Who Am I?
Who Are You?

Ideas and activities to explore both your
and young people's assumptions,
beliefs and prejudices

Jenny Nemko

RHP

Russell House Publishing

First published in 2006 by:
Russell House Publishing Ltd.
4 St. George's House
Uplyme Road
Lyme Regis
Dorset DT7 3LS
Tel: 01297-443948
Fax: 01297-442722
e-mail: help@russellhouse.co.uk
www.russellhouse.co.uk

© Jenny Nemko

A catalogue record for this book is available from the British Library.

British Library Cataloguing-in-publication Data:

ISBN: 1-903855-93-4
978-1-903855-93-5

Typeset by TW Typesetting, Plymouth, Devon
Printed by Alden Press, Oxford

About Russell House Publishing

RHP is a group of social work, probation, education and youth and community work practitioners and academics working in collaboration with a professional publishing team.

Our aim is to work closely with the field to produce innovative and valuable materials to help managers, trainers, practitioners and students.

We are keen to receive feedback on publications and new ideas for future projects.

For details of our other publications please visit our website or ask us for a catalogue. Contact details are on this page.

Contents

Acknowledgements   iv

Preface   v

Chapter 1 What's the Real Me?   1

Chapter 2 What am I for?   17

Chapter 3 Am I Really Alone?   31

Chapter 4 Why do Bad Things Happen?   42

Chapter 5 Is There a God?   56

Chapter 6 What Happens Next?   68

Chapter 7 What do I Believe?   77

Chapter 8 What About Spirituality?   98

Conclusion   110

Glossary   111

Resources   115

References and Useful Books   117

Acknowledgements

Judith Lyons inspired this book and made a specific contribution to Chapters one and six.

Angela Taylor was extremely generous with her time, offering invaluable suggestions and encouragement.

Pauline Webb, Paramjit Singh Kohli, the Venerable Sumana, Anisa Doha, Penny Grossman, Pam and Kamal Chawla contributed and checked information on the six faith traditions.

Vathani Mariampillai, Nikki Singh, Leigh Gordon, Monica and Daniel Joyce, Tenzin Chozom, Eva Grossman, Consey Demeester, Sahib Maker, Josh Brocklesby, Becca Citroen, Anish Narendran, Tanya Levene and others who wish to remain anonymous gave personal statements.

Dixon Upcott, Donald Chambers, Louise Kemp and Margaret McGeehan of the Harrow Youth Offending Service gave constructive criticism.

Friends, colleagues and young people read chapters, tried the exercises out and worked with me over the years.

Alan Taylor of Russell House commented wisely on the manuscript. Geoffrey Mann of Russell House supported me at every stage of the project. Martin Jones, Clive Newton and Peter Russell of Russell House eased the final stages of the project.

My husband Terry was with me all the way endlessly patient and loving.

For these many, many kindnesses much appreciation and a big thank you.

Preface

Who this book is for

This book is designed for anyone who is working with young people: workers, carers, leaders, advisers and teachers. It is written for the person who is affiliated to a faith group, for the person who is not affiliated and for the complete sceptic. It is intended for those who want to find out more about themselves and other people. Hopefully it will also help those who want to consider what spirituality is and what part it has to play in everyday life: work, leisure and relationships.

The aim of this book

There is an important yet often neglected dimension in many of our lives today. Although issues of personal health and social responsibility find a place in the media and in youth work of all sorts, the inner life, traditionally understood as spirituality, is rarely spoken of. In the home, in schools and in the wider community there is both a reticence and nervousness in discussing personal beliefs and values. We are not in the habit of asking questions like 'What do I really believe?' 'Do my actions reflect my beliefs?' 'What sort of person am I?' 'Why am I that sort of person?'

In our multi-faith and multi-cultural society we often know and work with people who come from very different backgrounds but rarely do we exchange ideas on what makes us tick. 'Why do you think like that?' 'What are your concerns?' 'What are your beliefs?' In fact, 'Who Are You?' And for that matter, 'Who Am I?'

With an interest to find out more, we – the professionals who work with young people – can influence the increasing gap between the religious and the secular way of life that results from a lack of knowledge on both sides. Even within a particular faith community it is often difficult to talk openly to a fellow believer. There can be a lack of communication between those who interpret their faith in different ways.

> We need to develop mutual knowledge, not just tolerance. The question is, what are you doing to find out about others? Respect comes out of knowledge; when you recognise my reality is as complex as yours, that's when you begin to know me and respect me.
>
> Hassan

What's missing in this debate is the very thing that can fill the gap – the development of a spiritual dimension to life: an awareness of common matters that over-ride and yet are part of both the religious and secular life style. Matters such as where we are going and what we are doing with our lives. Youth work has always been concerned with this spiritual dimension. From the days of the nineteenth century with the Young Men's Christian Association's (YMCA's) commitment to the 'improvement of the spiritual and mental condition of young men', through to the Secretary of State for Education and Employment, David Blunkett's pronouncement in 1998 that 'learning . . . helps make ours a civilised society, develops a spiritual side of our lives and promotes active citizenship' (NYA, 2005: 2), the subject of spirituality has been on the agenda. In 1999, the development of spirituality as part of a holistic approach to informal education became part of the National Occupational Standards:

> *Youth work addresses the development of the whole person, including social, spiritual, emotional, physical and intellectual education.*

> National Occupational Standards for Youth Work, from *Perspectives.* NYA, 1999: 5

In July 2005, the government published the green paper, *Youth Matters* in which spiritual development is clearly identified as part of what is anticipated will be included in the national standards on activities for young people (Clause 126 of *Youth Matters*, www.dfes.gov.uk/publications/youth). In preparation for this document, the National Youth Agency has produced a consultation paper that discusses the role of spirituality and spiritual development in youth work. The paper includes theoretical models for spiritual development and a discussion of the role of faith communities in developing spirituality and what spiritual development means in a secular or statutory setting (*Spirituality and Spiritual Development in Youth Work*, 2005, www.nya.org.uk).

The consultation paper also gives some general suggestions for activities in a secular setting with young people before concluding with a request for feed-back 'to be undertaken in a spirit of rigour and vigour' (2005: 27). As a result of this paper, the National Youth Agency hopes to find ways to explore spiritual issues on an individual basis as well as within a group work programme.

This, too, is my aim. One way is to start talking: to somehow generate deep, reflective conversation that allows people to consider their values and attitudes and to think about how these impact on themselves and on others. With this in mind, I decided to write a book that encourages young people to talk more openly, to question themselves and to listen to opinions that are different from their own. But I quickly realised that before we – the adult workers – can begin to encourage young people, we have to feel comfortable to talk about such matters ourselves. We have to give ourselves the chance to challenge our own assumptions, beliefs, instincts and prejudices. The chance to understand what influences and inspires us and perhaps to discover what it is that makes us who we are. Without going through this kind of process it is very easy to rely on other people to tell us who we are and to drift from one situation to the next.

Only when we have thought about and discussed these issues ourselves, will we be able to encourage young people to think for themselves. Then, we are able to educate in the real liberal sense of the word: in a way that opens minds and creates critical thinkers and helps us all to become life-long learners with control over our own destinies. Then, we are in a stronger position to curb the spread of extremist thought, speech and action that we are seeing in some sections of our society today.

What is in this book

There are two main strands running through every chapter in this book: Who Am I? – looking inwards at ourselves, and Who are you? – looking outwards at other people. Each chapter investigates one of the 'big questions' in life: what's the real me, am I really alone, is there a God, etc? Each chapter aims at an increasing awareness of our values and beliefs: our traditions and the traditions of others. People from a range of cultures and faith communities tell their stories and explain their journeys. Throughout the book there are Stop and Think Points, questionnaires and activities: some for you alone, others for you and your colleagues and still others for you, your colleagues and the young people with whom you work. Enlarging to an A4 size format is recommended when photocopying the questionnaires and handouts.

The book also provides a brief guide to some of the basic beliefs and practices of six major faith traditions and gives information on a few of the more popular secular philosophies. At the end of the book there is a glossary that defines many of the terms used in the text, a resource list of web-sites and a bibliography.

As you have probably already noticed, I will be speaking directly to you – as if you and I were sitting across the table talking together. This is the best way I know to get my message across.

How to use this book with young people

Spiritual development is part of the development of the whole of the young person, but even within a holistic approach, issues of spirituality cannot be raised apropos of nothing. This book aims to integrate a spiritual dimension into the work already being done with young people, whether within a group or on an individual basis.

First of all within a group, many of the thought starters and activities in Chapters 1 to 4 can be used as a part of, or as an extension to, the ad-hoc discussions and issue-based work that already takes place. For example, talk of stereotyping and of Black and Asian history fits in well with the activities in Chapter 1, 'What's the Real Me?' The second chapter, 'What Am I For?' presents practical ideas for ways in which young people can make a difference in their local and wider communities. Chapter 3, 'Am I Really Alone?' looks beneath social issues such as drug abuse and exclusion from school to suggest strategies for making loneliness a positive experience. The fourth chapter, 'Why Do Bad Things Happen?' addresses some of the difficulties that young people face and provides tips for moving on when bad things happen.

The last four chapters focus on personal values and beliefs. Chapters 5 to 7 explore the idea of learning about beliefs that we don't necessarily share. In conjunction with these chapters, family and friends can be invited to talk about their beliefs and how they affect their way of living. Chapter 8 introduces the idea of spirituality as an autonomous concept that is part of personal self-development, as well as a concept that is deeply rooted in religious identity.

On an individual basis, this book helps you to support young people when crises strike and good or bad things happen. A 'spiritual' response is one that gives space to the young person to think clearly and deeply: a response that involves empathy, listening and questioning skills. This kind of conversation does not happen without trust. Building trust is a slow process that takes time and is impossible to rush. You need to start where the person is at and gently encourage them to reflect privately upon the experience of day-to-day life. It often takes many conversations before they start to talk about their innermost feelings and say what is really on their mind. Before that, they may be protecting themselves and checking you, the listener, out. Pass the test by listening without judging. Good listening means active listening. You need to demonstrate that you are hearing and valuing what is being said.

When working with groups, there is a need to set boundaries, (see activity below) and consider how to deal with confidentiality, sarcasm, verbal and physical abuse. Even when you make the ground-rules clear, you may still have to deal with some difficult situations; disturbing issues may surface and you may find yourself trying to cope with revelations that give cause for concern. As, for example, when someone tells you about a recent incident of physical or emotional abuse at home. There may well be times when it is vital to call on professional help (such as qualified counsellors, mental health workers, drug workers, youth offending team, health centre representatives and GPs), who are able to deal with the issues that arise (Taylor, 2003: 20–5).

Activity: colleagues

Boundaries

Aim: To consider why boundaries are important, who they benefit and who they protect.

Method: Discuss what a boundary is. Take suggestions, from the participants, of the boundaries that they would like to establish for a group of colleagues, and for a group of young people. List on a flip chart.

Prompt List:

- Confidentiality
- Spreading gossip and rumours
- Telling jokes that may offend
- Wanting to come round to your home to talk
- Physical contact
- Racist or sexist language
- Abusive or aggressive behaviour
- Respect

Circle those boundaries that the group considers essential and discuss how realistic and possible it is to achieve those boundaries.

As well as respecting the boundaries of the people you are working with, there are your own boundaries to think about: how much you are prepared to self-disclose your own feelings and how much you wish to remain private. Sometimes, it is difficult to recognise our own emotions and comfort zones and know how to prevent our feelings getting out of control (see 'Telling My Story' in the activity section at the end of Chapter One). Again, professional help may be necessary.

For further information see: Taylor (2003) *Responding to Adolescence.* Lyme Regis: Russell House Publishing.

Where I am coming from

For many years, I have worked in a free-lance capacity for BBC Radio Religious Broadcasting. I present programmes and talks, often focusing on the common threads of spirituality found within many of the minority faith communities both in the United Kingdom and in the wider world. Alongside broadcasting, I run personal development training courses for young adults and professionals. I have become more and more aware of how much these two areas of work – personal and spiritual development – overlap. It seems to me that self-development is part of spiritual development for which there are few training courses!

I believe there is more to life than the material world. There is some other aspect that we do not understand; something that is indefinable, intangible and mysterious; something that perhaps is best described as spirituality. And what do I mean by that? Well, spirituality can be expressed in so many ways and perhaps it is easiest to start by saying what it isn't. Spirituality isn't cars, clothes and money and yet all these possessions can be imbued with spirituality. For example, using money to help to build a water system in a developing country has a non-material and a spiritual impact. A dimension of spirituality can be found in everything we do. At its most intense, spirituality for me is a feeling of wholeness and peace inside and at the same time a deep awareness that there is something beyond the physical body that we do not understand. It is the interconnectedness between the material world and the non-material world.

You may be wondering where organised religion comes into all this? Well, I think there is a difference between spirituality and religion, and that spirituality can be appreciated both within and without religion. And from time to time, we – those with a faith tradition and those without – all have the same instinctive sense of something more important than ourselves. It's a bit like the lanes on a motorway – in the fast lane life's whizzing past and we're busy with everyday life and haven't time to think. Occasionally we find ourselves in the inside lane in a frustrating bumper to bumper crawl but with a strong instinct that there is more to life than what we see, do and have.

To extend the metaphor, every philosophy, religion and way of life is a separate lane on the motorway – each to be valued and celebrated. Each lane contains the means to reach the same destination – to answer the same questions. So, because I have a Jewish background, and because I enjoy the Jewish dimension in my life, my particular lane on the motorway is Judaism. A way of life that gives me the tools to search for a spiritual element in everything I do. In the Jewish tradition, there's a Talmudic saying: 'This world is like a corridor before the world to come. Prepare yourself in the corridor so that you may enter the banquet hall.'

This doesn't necessarily mean an after-life. To me, it's like everyone's outside trying to get inside – perhaps, inside to our own souls or perhaps to the presence of God or maybe they're the same thing. Whatever . . . trying to get inside involves a wait in that corridor. But I don't think it has to be a patient, passive wait. For me, the wait's a struggle: a struggle to understand the non-material dimension in the day-to-day routine and a struggle to find out what is the point of living.

I am aware that my views and those of others presented in this book may be very different from yours. Some of the ideas may even annoy or offend you. But isn't it a useful exercise to step out of our own mind-sets and see things from another person's perspective? It's important for the atheist to recognise religion and for the religious to recognise atheism. It is part of the work we are doing: part of becoming aware of other people's deepest values. I certainly don't know the answers any more than you do. All I know is that one question leads inevitably to another; that a lack of self-questioning leads to complacency and that continuing to question is an important part of what it means to be a humane human being.

Chapter 1

What's the Real Me?

Each of us experiences ourselves at every moment of our waking lives, yet when it comes to knowing ourselves we are often unsure. Many times, our perception of others and ourselves is merely a stereotype, not a real person at all. Understanding a little more about how and why we think and act the way we do is a clue to who we really are. This, in turn, helps us to break down stereotypes, to look outwards and connect with the rest of the world.

This chapter looks at identity and in particular, the inner identity. It explores the many different parts that make up our identity and discovers how much the psychological, philosophical and religious view of the inner self have in common. It focuses on story telling as a tool for finding out what is the essential 'me'. In this chapter there are personal statements and questionnaires for you to do on your own. Throughout and at the end of the chapter, there are activities for you, your colleagues and the young people with whom you work.

Defining the Self

Labels

> I'm a Hindu hairdresser married to a Christian teacher from Algeria. I am a mother to my two-year old and a daughter to my seventy-year-old mother. I'm also a sister, a sister-in-law and an aunt.
>
> Poori

It is fairly easy to define ourselves using a simple label that describes name, age, sex, background, occupation, status within family and community, ethnic group, race and religion. But surely we are more than just these facts? There are others around with the same names as us, or with the same family status (father, mother, daughter, son) or with the same occupation that come from the same

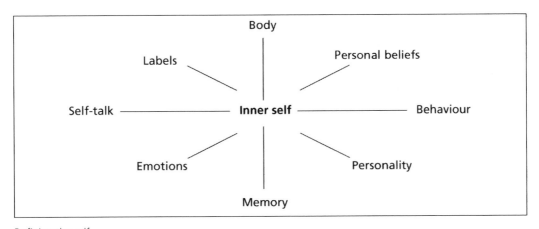

Defining the self

place. None of these labels really describe who we are. None of these labels are exclusively *us*. What is more, they may be simply labels that other people have decided to pin on us. Even our names, which seem a very personal expression of who we are, are usually the label that we were given at birth.

It doesn't always help to have a label.

I find that it's too dangerous to admit you're a 'care-leaver', that you haven't come from a family home. It's like having a dirty secret, or something that makes you 'different' in the inferior sense.

Bashmir

Often labels are used to pigeonhole an individual into a narrow category that does not reflect the real person. We have all at times over-heard people remarking that 'X are mean' or 'Y is stupid'. Such sweeping generalisations inevitably lead to stereotyping of the individuals in those particular groups.

I'm glad we're not dealing with that lot: they're all a load of losers.

Rhaneem

Activity: colleagues/young people

Label Me – 1

Aim: To explore the way labels are used.
Preparation: Write simple descriptions such as daughter, sister, teenager, student, school pupil, English, Indian, Christian, male, hairdresser, football supporter on each of approximately 25 luggage labels.
Method: Shuffle the labels and lay them face down in the middle of the circle. Take it in turns to pick up the top label and consider if the label is true for you and why. Talk about the way we label other people. Discuss the fact that how we think of ourselves is different sometimes from how others see us. Talk about the labels we have and the labels we would like to have.

Body

The way we look is an important part of our perception of ourselves and other people's perception of us. According to Albert Mehrabian's research, 57 per cent of the first impression we make on other people comes from what we look like, 36 per cent comes from how we sound and a mere 7 per cent comes from what we are actually saying (Argyle, 1991: 208).

Dipika has experienced being treated two different ways based on her two different ways of dressing:

I went into this smart grown-up type shop looking for something to wear to my brother's wedding. I was wearing my torn jeans and a scruffy old top . . . the assistant was really unhelpful, and I didn't buy anything. The next week I went back looking completely different: all done up . . . the same assistant obviously didn't recognise me because this time she was helpful and friendly and she helped me to find an outfit I like.

Dipika

Jonathan thinks his Territorial Army (TA) uniform gives the wrong impression to people who don't know him:

It's OK wearing the uniform when I'm with my mates at TA but it's embarrassing wearing it outside as some people look down at you without knowing anything about me and I don't like it when I feel people don't like me so I either change before I leave or I wear something on top.

Jonathan

Like Jonathan, Rahima experiences other people's negative impressions of her because of the clothes she wears. Nevertheless, her clothes are an important part of her identity and she continues to dress in the way she wants at all times. Rahima thinks that if she changes her clothes to fit in with other people's perception of her, she loses an important part of her self:

Although it's not always easy and sometimes I get shouted at on the street, I chose to wear a scarf and hijab . . . it's an important part of my identity . . . it means to me that I am dressing in a modest way that doesn't bring attention to my body and it makes me feel I belong.

Rahima

Sheila has just left prison. She knows that on the outside, people will be influenced by the way she looks. But, at the moment, she is unsure about herself and how she wants to dress:

Everyone in prison wears tracksuits. I've just come out and I don't have anything else. I have no idea what sort of image to go for. My mum took me shopping but I didn't know what I liked, I've come out a different person but I don't know who I am and what kind of clothes to buy.

Sheila

Activity: colleagues/young people

Label Me – 2

Aim: To explore how our perception of other people can be influenced by appearance

Preparation: Cut out a variety of pictures of people from teenage magazines.

Write an occupation on each of approximately 25 sticky labels (e.g. nursing, welding, car maintenance, hairdressing, accountancy, shop work, youth work, legal work).

Write a leisure activity on each of approximately 25 sticky labels (e.g. gym, football, watching TV, canoeing, reading, CDs., travelling).

Write a positive, negative or neutral personal quality on each one of approximately 25 sticky labels (e.g. shy, bossy, talkative, quiet, brave, jealous, angry, kind, enthusiastic, bored, disappointed, helpful, friendly, unfriendly, unhelpful, rude, polite, pleasant, interested, under-confident, cruel, cowardly, bully, fair, stupid, depressed, funny, generous, racist).

Also have available large sheets of paper and paste.

Method: Pick a 'cut-out person' and stick on a large sheet of paper.

Decide on occupation, leisure activity and personal qualities and use stickers accordingly.

In discussion afterwards, talk about why we think 'cut-out person' does that particular job, enjoys that particular leisure activity and has those particular personal qualities. Ask questions such as 'which of these people is the bossy one?' and 'what is it that makes someone appear to be bossy?'

Discuss the assumptions made on the basis of body image. How come we have a definite perception although we really do not know what the person does for a living, etc?

Conclude, if appropriate on a more personal note by connecting personal confidence with body image. Being in tune with our appearance is part of feeling confident. It helps to observe others and our own body language: the way we sit and stand, the way we hold our heads, facial expression and eye contact. Note how much space we take around us.

If appropriate, extend the discussion by talking about how we sound. According to Mehrabian's research discussed earlier, 36 per cent of the first impression we make on other people comes from the voice. Talk about pitch, pace, how loudly and how quietly we speak (Morrison, 2001: 4–13).

Personal Beliefs

Our parents, carers and teachers are the source of many of our beliefs about the outside world and about ourselves. Opinions such as 'you're stupid' or 'you're a born artist' can become facts. They aren't really facts at all. They are perceptions formed by experience and the views of others. Some beliefs are enabling and some are limiting. An enabling belief allows us to feel confident and possibly reach our goals whereas a limiting belief leads to lack of motivation and less chance of success.

Enabling belief

I exercise and keep fit, because there is a purpose to this. I put my full attention and energy into the game and I have the potential to win any match I play.

Ronnie

Limiting belief

I ended up doing what I didn't want to do and I've been thinking about it. Why do I never say what I really want? I think it's down to my childhood. My mother always used to say, 'I wants don't get' whenever I said 'I want' . . . and I've always believed it.

Julie

Our beliefs about ourselves influence our thoughts. As a practical example of this, there are many scientific studies in which someone is hypnotised and told that an everyday object such as a pen is exceptionally heavy. When the person is brought out of a trance, they find it impossible to lift the pen. Electronic measures show that one part of the body, the person's biceps, is expending energy to lift the pen. However, another part of the body, the triceps, is unconsciously working harder to stop the pen being lifted. This is because the hypnotist has planted a belief of being unable to lift the pen. There is a strong unconscious drive to behave consistently with our beliefs.

Complete this questionnaire in order to gain insight into your beliefs about yourself.

Beliefs questionnaire

Complete these sentences:

   I am good at . . .

   I am not good at . . .

Consider your beliefs in your capacity as a manager, trainer or whatever role you have at work and write a brief response to each of the following:

   What do you believe is your role at work?

   What do you believe are your strengths and weaknesses in that role?

   What are your beliefs about the capability of your colleagues/the people you manage?

Self-talk

Self-talk is determined by our beliefs about ourselves and directly influences our behaviour. Self-talk is the stream of consciousness that goes through our heads all the time. Observe your own thinking for a moment, and you will see that it is an ever-changing stream of consciousness. One thought pops into your mind, suggests another, which in turn suggests another, and off you go on a roller-coaster of associations, often ending up with no recollection of the particular thought that started it all off.

Again, as with our personal beliefs, self-talk can be either positive or negative.

Negative self-talk

I'm not nearly as good as he is . . . he always gets it right . . . I don't think I can do it at all at the moment . . . maybe I could if I really wanted to have a try . . . I don't know and I don't really think so.

Kandip

Positive self-talk

I'm not pleased with the way that worked out but it's a one-off. I'll be much better next time.

Refullah

Behaviour

The way we act gives an indication to others of the sort of people we are inside. Sometimes there is a contradiction between what we say and how we act. For example, we may say to a friend 'I'm going to be at home this evening so come over whenever you want'. Then another friend phones and we agree to go out to the cinema without letting our first friend know.

Stop and Think: you/colleagues

Behaviour is the part of our identity that is on show all the time. How we behave affects other people as well as ourselves. This questionnaire aims to make you more aware of the difference between the person you think you are and the way you behave.

1. You have applied for a job you really want and you don't have all the necessary qualifications. Would you lie on your CV?
   Yes, if I felt it would get me an interview for the job ☐
   Certainly not ☐
   Of course, everybody does it ☐
2. You have bought more than the legal amount of alcohol when abroad. Would you still pass through the 'nothing to declare' customs area?
   I'd probably take a chance ☐
   No way ☐
   Yes, it works every time ☐
3. A faulty cash machine has given you £200 too much. Would you report it?
   No, it wasn't my fault I was given too much ☐
   Yes, if I had time to do so ☐
   Yes, I would feel uncomfortable keeping the money ☐
4. When you are on holiday with a friend, you find their diary half hidden under some clothing. Would you read it?
   I'd like to read it, but I feel they are entitled to their privacy ☐
   Yes, they won't mind as they tell me what they're doing anyway ☐
   Yes, I've been concerned about what they have been up to lately ☐
5. You find out that your partner of two years is having an affair. What do you do?
   It would be hard, but I would forgive them ☐
   I would trash their car or something else that really mattered to them ☐
   No hesitation, I'd dump them ☐

Emotions

Our emotions such as anger, worry, inhibition, feeling hurt, happiness, excitement and satisfaction can change as rapidly as our thoughts. Open a letter one morning that tells you that you've just won a fortune and you'll feel pleased and excited. Open the next letter that tells you it was all a mistake and you'll feel disappointed and miserable:

> *I'm so upset. My brother promised he'd get me into the game and I rushed everything so I could be ready to go. I just did it all in time and now he's phoned to say he wants to take his girl friend. It's just so unfair.*

Lester

And on a much larger scale, consider how you felt on the 6th July 2005 when you heard Britain's Olympic bid was successful compared to how you felt the very next day when four bombs exploded in London killing over 50 innocent people:

In a matter of 24 hours my emotions went up and down like being on a rollercoaster. When I heard the Olympic Games are coming to Britain in 2012, I felt great . . . really pleased for Britain and for London. The next day when the bombs hit, I was frightened and sad.

Joshua

Memory

What we remember affects our thoughts, attitudes and actions. Yonni's memories don't always help her to feel good about herself but they make her realise who she really is:

The fact that I remember some of the things I've done in the past and a lot of the bad things that have happened to me is horrible sometimes. I want to forget sometimes but then I think of some of the good things as well and I know that all my memories are the real me.

Yonni

That's fine but what happens if we lose our memory? Would we cease to be 'the real me'?

Five years ago I was knocked over by a van while crossing the road. I lost consciousness and remained in a coma. When I came round days later in a hospital intensive care unit, I had lost my memory. So I had in effect lost my identity. I was suddenly all-but-dead meat. So who am I now? A year ago I began piecing together what happened to me and my memories helped me a little and now I realise how much I depend on memory for my identity that makes me who I am. I've relied on the help of family and friends and strangers to try to understand my memories.

Lubi

But even if you haven't lost your memory, it is often hard to rely on memory for an accurate account of what has happened. You may think that your memory stretches way back into childhood, an unbroken record of the person you are. But try talking to a friend about something you have done together. No two accounts are exactly the same!

Now try and remember in detail even what happened yesterday. Or harder still what happened in detail on any particular day last week. Try and remember what you were doing on 1st September last year . . . so what do you remember? Once we start delving into the past in this way, we find that if our sense of self depends upon memory, then we must be like a jigsaw with some of the pieces missing.

Personality

My personality is different from my sisters' personality. I'm the only person who has the personality that I have. My personality's quite bouncy and outgoing. My sister's more placid and quiet.

Joel

When we dig deeper, we become aware of both the conscious and the unconscious elements of the personality. The personality includes what goes on in the mind as well as the outward behaviour. Psychologists have explored the personality in order to help people to understand themselves as individuals.

There are many theories about the personality. One is the 'nurture/environment' theory. A theory that presents the personality as the outcome of how we were brought up from birth. This means that babies are virtually 'blank slates', upon which parents and society write. In this view there is no personality that exists prior to social interaction and the personality is wholly dependent on the environment.

Another theory is known as the 'nature/genetics' theory. This theory takes on board hereditary characteristics and questions whether such characteristics form the basis of the individual's mature personality in later life. For example, some research has shown that 12 week old babies have certain characteristics such as friendliness and fussiness that continue into adolescence (Fontana, 1992: 168):

> *Well I could tell you who I am: like my name's Leigh, I'm 18 years old and things like that. Or I could say why I am who I am. I believe that my inner 'me' – the way I act, the people I hang out with and the way I dress – is a product of both nurture and nature, environment and genetics.*

Leigh

Freud's psychological view on personality

Sigmund Freud (1856-1939) in one of his theories on personality acknowledges that there are deep layers of personality: parts of us that exist beyond what we can really know. He uses the terms super-ego (conscious mind), ego (pre-conscious mind) and id (unconscious mind).

1. Super-ego: this is our awareness of everyday matters known as consciousness. What we do, think and decide and how we interact with the world around us. It is our experience of each day, with thoughts like, 'She asked me to do this, and I said I would' or 'I'm really looking forward to going away' or 'try and remember to collect the clothes on your way home'.
2. Ego: this contains a great deal of information and details in the form of recorded memories, both experienced and imagined. This layer of awareness consists of the things we may not actively be aware of in the moment. Some of these things are easily retrievable such as our very recent memories and even the sounds going on around us right now. Others are more hidden. The information in this level of our minds is potentially but not always accessible to super-ego. Ego information can be accessed via various contemplative and hypnotic techniques carried out by qualified professionals.
3. Id: this is part of the mind with which we are all born. The contents of this part of the mind cannot under normal circumstances be brought to consciousness. It is full of timeless images, memories, animal instincts and genetic tendencies. From the id entire worlds are created and destroyed during the night when we dream. The id also motivates our behaviour, beliefs, and experiences in mysterious ways. In the id many levels of communication take place, all at once – most are far beyond conscious comprehension. Freud calls it 'chaos, a cauldron of seething excitations' (Freud, 1991: 106).

The inner self

When we hear or read about people who have survived extraordinary circumstance, these individuals usually say that it was their spirit – something inside themselves – that helped them to carry on. Terry Waite was taken hostage in Lebanon and remained imprisoned for nearly five years, four of which were in solitary confinement. He was chained to a wall, often left in darkness, beaten and subjected to mock executions:

> *I had no books or papers or radio for a very long time. And of course, no conversation with any other person. I had to learn how to live from within. I learned to be able to draw on inner*

resources, and I discovered that in fact the unconscious can and will come to our aid in situations of extremity and difficulty . . . I felt alone and isolated. But I could say in the face of my captives, you had the power to bend my mind, and you tried, the power to break my body, and you've tried, but my soul, my spirit is not yours to possess.

Terry Waite, www.bbc.co.uk/onthisday/hi/witness

Many psychologists, philosophers and religious thinkers suggest that coming to know ourselves leads to increased peacefulness and personal freedom.

Often the hardest part of ourselves to understand is our innermost self – our essence – the core of being that has been with us since we were born and that is absolutely unique to us. This is the part of our identity that no-one sees and very few people know about:

It's difficult to talk about but if I was to call anything an 'inner, inner me' it would be the things that I am not fully aware of.

Leigh

It is useful to know and understand ourselves if we want to understand others. It is not necessary to feel positive about every aspect of our personalities but it is possible to feel more comfortable with ourselves.

Stop and Think: you/colleagues

To gain an insight into your inner feelings, make a list of at least four items for each category. It doesn't matter if there are replications in the lists. This is not about compiling numerous facts, but about looking at yourself in different ways:

- good qualities you possess
- areas in your personality that might need improvement
- personal ambitions
- things about yourself that you particularly like
- things about yourself that you would want to keep secret from others
- unique selling points about yourself
- bad habits and why you do them
- personal prejudices and why you have them
- ways in which you enhance the world you live in
- subjects that interest you passionately
- possessions you desire
- types of people that attract you

Now go back over your lists and edit them for truth. Cross out any that you do not truly believe, even if this reduces your answers below the minimum of four. When you are satisfied that these represent an honest view of yourself, use the information you have gathered to write a 300 word appraisal of 'the real you' – the person and your present life.

In this next section, we look at what philosophy and religion have to say about the inner self, known in philosophical and theological language as the soul.

The Ancient Greek philosophical view of the soul

The Greek philosophers defined the soul in many ways. According to Plato (c.428–c.348 BCE) the soul is a disembodied spiritual being that can exist independently of all matter and all things except God. The soul is the source of the real person, self or consciousness. And the soul is the source of all that is the best and good.

According to one of Aristotle's (384–322 BCE) ideas, everything that lives including plant and animal life has a soul. The human soul is different in that it has a rational faculty (a mental power than can reason) that not only recognizes but also can discriminate between good and bad (Angeles, 1992: 287-8).

A religious view of the soul

There is a great similarity between philosophical and theological teachings on the soul. For example, the philosopher Plotinus (c.205–270) explained that in the beginning of existence the soul had to descend to the body. This idea is similar to the religious idea of union between God (the soul) and Humanity (the body). The human soul is viewed as the part of the human self that is divine (of God) and is therefore, actually or potentially united to God. The soul desires union with God and the search for the divine connection between the soul and God involves a mystical journey that passes through the dense, material world to the light, ethereal world of the divine.

The mystical journey is a universal concept and does not belong to any one religion. Most religions, both Western and Eastern, have mystical traditions. Within many of these traditions reflection, meditation and prayer are stages on the way towards union with the One or God. These stages often involve learning to control material 'needs' in order to feed spiritual 'needs' – the needs of our inner, private life. In mystical terms the soul or inner self is a divine spark of God that longs to return to God.

In some ways, the mystical path translates into Freudian terms. The goal is to control and ultimately to eradicate the super-ego. Taking the mystical path is a gradual journey that departs from the super-ego, passes through the ego and arrives at the id – the part of the mind that we are born with. Perhaps the id is the inner self or the soul.

Using storytelling to find the 'real me'

Mystical journeys may not be the answer at the moment to find out 'What's the Real Me?' A more practical way to begin maybe is to remember where we have come from, what we have done with our lives, the influences we have experienced – in fact, to try to identify where we are in our story on our journey so far.

Most of us love stories and have done so as far back as we can remember. We may have listened to family stories – older people recounting family gossip, scandal and wisdom. We may have been surrounded by stories in the rhymes, games and jingles of the street and the playground. Some of us probably made up our own stories too. Everything, from what we did last night to what we would do if given three magic wishes, is food for the human instinct for story telling.

Why? Because imagination is one of the best tools we have for asking questions about life and trying out various answers. When we construct a story, we have to say *In the beginning . . .* or *If this happened, then that might follow . . .* or *What if this had happened instead . . .* or *That happened because . . .* or *If only . . .*

So we use our logic, **our reason, our em**pathy and our ability to speculate.

We need to tell stories in order to organise our experience as well as to pass our experience on to others and in order to explore the meaning of our lives. As soon as we tell someone about something that has happened to us – or we'd like to happen to us – we're telling a story. We're putting experience or fears or longings into words, and the words can make it 'real' for someone else, or even for ourselves! Being in a fight isn't the same as telling the story of it later, but the story, not the event as it happened, will be usually where we work out why the fight happened and how we feel about it. It will also be the only form in which anyone else can 'experience' the fight.

We don't yet fully understand the connections between thought and language, but some psychologists believe that we can only think what we can say. Whether or not this is true, there is agreement that the process of putting things into words gives us more control over our experience. Of course, 'control' is a dangerous thing. As we tell our story we choose, maybe subconsciously, what to include and what to leave out, what to gloss over and what to highlight. Literature is full of 'unreliable narrators', and modern novelists in particular, like to play with the possibilities of alternative versions of events, challenging the reader about which one to trust. The excitement of TV courtroom dramas and most whodunits depends on witnesses' conflicting evidence. Because of this, the words 'story' and even 'history' are notoriously ambiguous.

Recording an event gives it permanence. You can read first-hand accounts of love and war from years ago; the lovers and soldiers are gone but their stories remain. It does not matter that you cannot assess the 'reliability' of their accounts. The stories have their own life now – separate from that of the events they record. Every time we read them, the events are recreated in us. And our re-living of them will be different from another reader's.

The following two activities focus on our personal stories, how much we are prepared to disclose to others and the extent to which belonging to a group gives us a sense of who we are.

Group activities: colleagues/young people

Telling my story

Aim:	To identify personal characteristics, to consider the degree to which you want other people, including the young people you work with, to know about you.
Idea:	Telling your own story is rather like dropping a stone in a pond. The first few ripples are close and visible but as the circle widens the ripples are less obvious. Towards the edge they disappear altogether.
	When you meet some-one for the first time and they ask you who you are, you probably are willing to tell them a few 'safe' facts – your name, where you live and what you do. These facts represent the visible ripples in the middle of the pond. As you get to know the person better you are likely to speak more openly about yourself – your likes and your dislikes. Eventually you may trust them with your innermost feelings – your dreams and your fears. Your dreams and fears represent the mysterious undefined ripples at the edge of the pool. Unless you look carefully you can hardly see them at all.
Preparation:	Photocopy the handout of the three questions and the drawing of a many-rippled pond.
Method:	Talk through idea.
	Complete the photocopied drawing of 'many-rippled pond'.

Discuss how many ripples of the pond you are prepared to talk about with the young people you work with. Talk about how you cope with inappropriate questions about your private life.

Many Rippled Pond and the Three Questions Handout

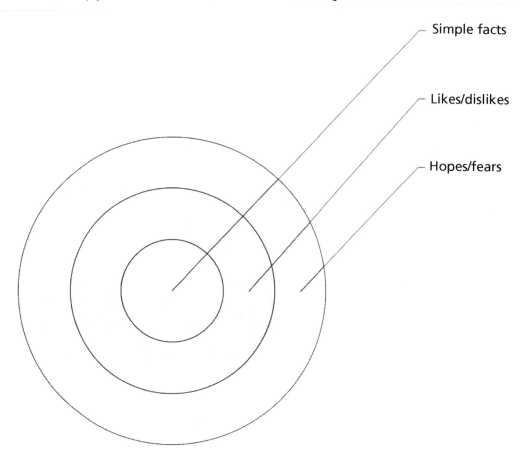

Simple facts

Likes/dislikes

Hopes/fears

It may be helpful to think about these questions whilst completing the diagram

1. If someone you don't know asks you about yourself, what would you say?

2. If someone you do know asks you about yourself, what would you say?

3. If someone you like and trust asks you about yourself, what would you say?

Group Activity: colleagues/young people

Who do you think you are?

Aim: To consider the extent to which belonging to a group gives you a sense of 'who you are.'

Preparation: Photocopy the chart for each participant.

Method: Use the chart to grade the group according to how much it helps give you a sense of 'who you are'. Discuss why a particular grade was given. Do you feel that one group more than any other give you a sense of 'who you are'? Or do you feel that you belong to a mixture of groups? How far do you think it is important to mix with people from many different groups?

Chart to photocopy: Who do you think you are?

Group	Grade out of ten	Why that grade
Family		
Friendship group		
Age group		
Sports group		
Music group/fan group		
Interest group, e.g. T.A. (Territorial Army)		
Religious group		
Languages you speak		
Political party/views		
Ethnic group		
Nationality		
Any other groups		

Adapted from *Dealing with Conflict*, Wedell, 2006.

The last two activities in this chapter focus on the important events and influences in our lives. Both activities can be tackled independently or with your colleagues in pairs or in small groups. Although the activities can also be used with a young person on a one-to-one basis or in a small group, caution is advised. It is essential to assess whether or not the activity may prove too intrusive at this moment in time.

Activity: you/colleagues/young people

Meaningful events

Aim: To think about the important events in our lives, the effect those events have on our thinking now and how much we want to disclose to the young people we work with.

Using non-verbal means such as a 'time and events line' diagram may make it easier to express our thoughts before we begin to explain these ideas to someone else.

Method: Photocopy the 'time and event line' drawing for each person.

Working alone, insert both positive and negative events that have been and are important. This can be done in drawing or writing.

If working in pairs, take it in turns to discuss the events on your charts. Limit interruptions and comments when the other person is speaking allowing thinking space to formulate views and to think about the subject from a personal perspective. There may well be feelings to off-load that will assist to clarify thoughts.

When everyone has shared events, you may want to come together as a group to exchange views on the effect past events have on your thinking now.

These life events form the basis of a discussion on where you are right now, what is 'the real you' and your hopes and fears for the future. If in discussion, it is useful to remind those who are eager to speak to leave space for others who may be less forthcoming.

Time and Event Handout

Events:			
Father wanted a boy	Went to school I wanted to go to Failed exam	First boyfriend Got job	Have a beautiful baby Money problems
Baby	**Child**	**Teens**	**Twenties**

Time
0–3 yrs
3–6 yrs
6–12 yrs
12–13 yrs
13–14 yrs
15–16 yrs
16–17 yrs
17–18 yrs
18–20 yrs
20–25 yrs

Activity: colleagues/young people

Heroes and Heroines

Aim: To think about the way we want to live our lives.

Idea: This activity encourages us to get in touch with our real feelings about what's going on in and outside of us. It is from the people who influence us most that we often draw our values for life. What do we learn about ourselves by following their example? If we look at why they inspire us we may be able to recognise what it is in life that we are looking for. In discovering this, we can begin to develop our own potential instead of depending on someone else to fulfil our dreams.

Method: Ask the group to think about their favourite character. It may be someone from a recent film, the pop star business, a world figure, a close friend or a relative.

In pairs, tell each other about that person. Are they male or female? Young, old? Strong, gentle, kind? Adventurous, brave, good-looking?

Return to the group to discuss. Point out any similarities in the pairs' choice of character.

Ask about any similarities between the individual and their chosen character. How are they like their hero and heroine? What do they admire? How much is this role model good for them? How is this person unhelpful to them? Are they happy trying to be like them?

(Adapted from *The Space Between*, Mountain, 2004)

Chapter 2

What am I for?

This chapter looks at what gives our day-to-day life a sense of purpose and meaning: what we want to have and what we want to be. It talks about people who have found purpose in life. Finally, it considers the possible purpose of life beyond our everyday experience and how we can personally make a difference.

Throughout the chapter, there are questionnaires and personal development exercises. Some are designed for you alone, others are designed for you and your colleagues in self-development training workshops. For young people, there is a suggested series of sessions that promote positive action in the community.

Purpose in our day-to-day life

Basic physical needs for human existence must be acknowledged before we can consider higher needs like giving purpose and meaning to our day-to-day life. First we need the essential material things – air, water, food and shelter – that no one can survive without or at least not for long. Certainly, for the starving person, food becomes the highest priority and for the homeless, a search for shelter dominates.

But what it means to be a human being rarely stops there. The list of basic physical needs includes a number of much more intangible needs: our emotional, mental and spiritual needs. Maslow's theory of Hierarchy of Needs examines this process in detail (Barnes, 2002: 33). Often at the same time as coping with the basic necessities, we puzzle over the purpose of our lives. And once we are fed, clothed and have somewhere to live, the search to satisfy our needs becomes a major preoccupation:

I don't know what I want to do in my life . . . I just know I want it to mean something to me.

Ranin

Most people want to be happy and if you ask them what will make them happy, they will quite often give a list of material possessions: the perfect body, a fast car, an exciting holiday, a high paying job. The underlying assumption is that to have these things will somehow also lead to deeper love, more esteem from friends and a greater sense of fulfilment. Yet, more and better material goods do not automatically translate into a more satisfying, happy and purposeful life:

Buying stuff doesn't help . . . going out doesn't help . . . I just keep getting the feeling that everything's pointless . . . there's no purpose to anything . . . I don't know why I'm feeling like this . . . there's nothing much worth living for and I'm worth nothing.

Ben

So where are you right now? What is your situation? Are your relationships and your work meaningful? What purpose does your life have at the moment? What are your strengths and weaknesses? What is your place in the wider world? In order for us to help young people to think about these questions, it is necessary for us – the people who work with young people – to clarify our own sense of purpose.

We may feel in a rut, unable to see further than the next day, living without the expectation of new and exciting things, or it may be just the opposite. The strange thing is that we all instinctively know when something is not how we believe it should be and it is this state that leads us to internal civil war: that constant inner feeling of conflict which cannot quite be resolved. It is this 'dis-ease' that can cause such deep-seated dissatisfaction with our very existence that we can begin the process of self-destruction.

Working with the premise that nothing happens in the outside world before it takes place in the mind means that what we are and what we will become is subject to our thoughts and belief structures. It is natural therefore that we operate in life within our own set of parameters often never straying beyond the limits imposed by our own beliefs.

The glass ceiling

Some time ago this idea was developed into a concept of the 'glass ceiling', The idea of the 'glass ceiling' is that our beliefs act as a ceiling, a limit of expectation which places a boundary to any and all parts of our lives – income, state of health, happiness, social status, self worth, etc. We may be able to see where we want to get to but in attempting the climb we encounter the 'glass ceiling' and stop and turn back.

Many of our beliefs, values and a large part of our individual identity are moulded by a process of socialisation, of growing up, finding our place in the order of things and becoming part of the community. Who we are and what part we feel able to play in the larger scheme of things begins to form in our minds at a very early age and continues throughout most of our lives.

Socialisation of the individual is a very complex and subtle process taking many forms yet it has been likened to the training of a flea. As you probably know, the flea can jump to tremendous heights relative to its size. That is a problem if you happen to be a flea circus owner or indeed a member of the audience! So, to eliminate this problem the fleas' behaviour has to be modified in some way and for this purpose they are put into a box on which is placed a glass lid.

At first the fleas continue to jump and of course in doing so hit their heads on the glass ceiling resulting in a painful lesson. After a very short time the fleas will stop jumping so high, in fact to just within a fraction of an inch below the glass and from that time onwards will never, even with the glass removed out-jump that height set by the now internalised ceiling on their existence.

In the case of the human being the glass ceiling is put in place by our subjective experiences of life, by society, by our parents and carers, by our teachers and by ourselves. The glass ceiling is often fixed by the painful experiences of life. And pain levels at an early age can appear much worse than later on in life. This would seem to explain the greater effect of early experiences that add up to a belief structure which runs our lives in an almost totally automatic subconscious way. Once in place we will never out-perform our ceiling, however hard we try our beliefs will always triumph. What we can do is modify the belief structure or move the ceiling height to a higher setting and thus increase our potential. In fact the mere acknowledgement of the existence of this self-perpetuating ceiling can begin the process of change.

Stop and Think: you

What is your glass ceiling set at, what are your expectations of life, what limitations are you placing on yourself? Jot down your evaluation of your own situation next to the items in the following list:

State of health	excellent/good/average/sickly/bad
State of happiness	ecstatic/good/reasonable/average/glum
Max income level	£
Self-confidence	totally confident/somewhat confident/unsure
Class	upper/middle/working
Learning ability	clever/average/below average
Manual dexterity	able/average/ham fisted
Artistic ability	adept/inept
Social skills	I fit in most places/feel ill at ease sometimes/always
Ability to make friends	easily/some difficulty/awkward
Luck	very lucky/somewhat lucky/no luck at all
Sports	competitive/non competitive
Self worth	high/average/lowish

You now have an insight into where you are right now in regards to the perception you have about yourself and in regards to where your glass ceiling level is set. This exercise can also be used to help young people assess their perception of themselves.

Recalling the positive experiences we have had in the past can influence our actions in the present and help us to make decisions about what we want in the future. The following 'Positives' exercise raises awareness of some of your achievements and encourages positive thinking.

Positives

Try to remember the occasions when you did well, when good things happened. List the particular skills used and the good feelings experienced and anything else really positive. For example, 'yesterday I went to see my supervisor and I told her exactly how I felt. I was really pleased because I'd felt for ages that I wanted to say something'.

The list usually takes several attempts to develop. Try to add to it day by day. Patiently and persistently question yourself. Then on a daily basis simply read it through and actively recall your positives for a few minutes. Keep a copy for future reference.

Stop and Think: you

Affirmations

Here is an exercise that can help you focus on the personal qualities you would like to have and how you would like to be perceived by other people.

Write about four to six positive statements about yourself on separate cards. Write the statement down as if you already have the specific quality that you want to have in the future. State precisely what you want rather than what you don't want.

Make sure each short sentence is in the present tense: e.g. 'I always listen' rather than 'I will listen'; is personal: e.g. 'I am always confident in all situations'; is positive: e.g. 'I am very co-ordinated when I play netball' rather than 'I sometimes miss a goal when I play netball'.

Read each affirmation aloud twice a day. This should only take 10–20 seconds per affirmation (only a couple of minutes or so per day).

As you read imagine:

- What you would see.
- What you would hear.
- What you would feel.

Examples of affirmations

I enjoy dancing and I'm a good dancer and I'm going to dance school as soon as I've got the money together.

I do a tasty sausage, egg and chips and people like coming to my place and having a meal with me.

I help with the younger kids from time to time and I always think about what they want to do.

I'm a good laugh and my friends and me have a good time when we go out together.

I like my shiny black leather jacket and I feel I look good when I wear it.

I do regular exercise and I'm really fit and I am playing a lot of sport and I am doing very well at it.

Setting goals

Now you have an idea of the personal qualities you would like to have, you can start to go about it by setting yourself some goals. The following pointers help with setting goals:

- Define precisely and describe what your ideal world or lifestyle will be three years from today.
- Check that your description is balanced. Ensure that you have covered every important aspect of your life.
- Check that your description is precise. If you want a fast car, then name it and describe its year, colour, mileage, etc. and what you will see, hear and feel when you are successful.
- Check that your description is challenging and stretching.
- Check that your description is desirable – that it is what you really want.
- Once you have fully completed points 1-5 repeat them for one-year goals always ensuring that you identify the milestones needed if you are to achieve your three-year goals.
- Repeat the process for six months, three months, and one-week goals. Look again at your list after a couple of days. If necessary, refine it.

The goal setting process takes time and does not need to be done in one go. Each goal needs to be broken down into bite-size pieces. For example, if you want to have changed jobs in 12 months' time, think of smaller goals like carrying out a skills review by the end of this month, revising your CV by the end of next month and identifying and applying for five vacancies by the end of six months.

Regularly review your goals: at least weekly but ideally every day. This will only take five to ten minutes a day. Despite the small amount of time required reviewing goals, many people find it difficult to find the time. Try it out yourself. Notice how easy or difficult you find this activity. Once you have worked through the goal setting process, you may wish to encourage the young people you work with to do likewise. They may wish to keep their general goals and aspirations private. However, it is worth discussing with them how high a priority are their goals and what is the substance of the goals?

Of course, goals can change or not be achieved in the time set. There are often outer (outside you) and inner (inside you) obstacles to overcome. Below are some outer and inner obstacles together with some possible solutions for you to think about.

Outer obstacles to achieving goals

Other people

Other people can be a major obstacle to achieving goals. A real difficulty can arise from friends and colleagues. They can sometimes undermine you. The process of this undermining may be crude. You may be told 'You'll never make it' or 'You're a loser'. It can also be far subtler like 'Don't set your goals too high or you'll be disappointed if you don't get there'. These people are giving you a negative affirmation. In work teams, sometimes teasing by team-mates is very negative. Other people may discourage you because they make no attempt to encourage you. Yet others may want to distract you and encourage you to do other things, or suggest that there are different priorities.

Solutions to 'other people'

Techniques of detachment and rational analysis can help you to counteract other people's behaviour.

Detachment

A sense of detachment; that is a distancing of yourself from unpleasant feelings is an effective way of dealing with destructive emotions and of combating external stress. One such technique is as follows:

1. Think of a time when you were stressed or had strong negative thoughts or feelings.
2. Imagine stepping out of your body leaving behind all those responses.
3. Notice how you become calmer, cooler and more rational, as you undertake point 2.

Having done points 1–3 for a minute or two, return to point 1. Notice how you can keep a sense of detachment while returning to this point.

Rational analysis

This technique is excellent because it challenges people to think differently. It is useful if the detachment technique can be mastered first, then you can go into an analysis of yourself or of other people. The key points of the analysis are as follows:

- Be specific and do not allow any generalisations.
- Set objective measurable criteria for judgements.
- Prove objectively and measurably what is being said.
- Write these things down.

Once you have cleared any of your own irrational beliefs or feelings you can introduce these techniques into your sessions with young people. If you do this for five to ten minutes each session you can significantly undermine negative perspectives.

Stress

Stress is another widespread obstacle to achieving goals. This comes from a wide range of external life changing events. Perhaps the most negative examples are bereavement and divorce. Happy events like promotion to a new job may also be extremely stressful in that it may mean moving home, finding somewhere to live, settling yourself and your family into the area and getting on with new work colleagues.

Solutions to stress

Relaxation and visualisation are valuable antidotes to stress. A particular piece of music that gives you a positive feeling can also help you to get rid of stress. Other techniques that may be helpful include detachment (see above).

Sometimes the stress level is very high and professional help is required.

Relaxation

Relaxation is a good general technique. It is an excellent preparation for many of the mental exercises. This is one example of a relaxation process:

- Get in a comfortable sitting or lying position in a quiet place.
- Focus on your breathing.
- Breathe through your nose as if smelling a flower.
- Release the breath very slowly through the mouth on a 'sh' sound.
- Notice the rhythm of your breathing.
- Compare the level of relaxation in different parts of your body, hands versus shoulders, legs versus arms, neck versus feet, etc.
- Allow this to go on for two to three minutes.
- Either continue this process or add the technique of visualisation by visualising a positive past experience or a future positive experience (see below under Visualisation).

Visualisation

This is also called mental imagery or imaging. The aim is to bring to mind how it feels to achieve your goal. Effective visualisation includes what is seen, heard, felt (by touch and emotions), smelt and tasted. With practice visualisation becomes easier. You can visualise effectively by following this list:

- Sit comfortably and let your body relax. If you are tense your muscles get contradictory messages.
- Think of one of your specific goals and create a successful outcome in your head.
- Use all your senses. Remember that visualisation is not just seeing with the mind's eye, but also touching, tasting, smelling and recalling how it feels emotionally to perform in this way.
- Practise regularly. Five minutes a day, once a day, for ten days is a good start.

Inner obstacles to achieving goals

Negative memories and expectations

Negative memories and expectations are both common inner obstacles to achieving goals. Think about your own experiences and those of the people you work with. You will hear many people with negative expectations. They will talk about these negative outcomes and make them more likely to happen. In your case, you may project a negative expectation of your future. You anticipate the worst possible outcome. A particular job, colleague or future event causes you to think about a negative outcome. This outcome comprises negative self-talk, images and feelings.

Linked to negative expectations are negative memories. Negative memories of bad experiences may be triggered by a particular event or venue. The negative memory will lead to negative self-talk (the stream of unconscious thoughts that fill our heads) and feelings of low self-esteem.

Solutions to negative memories and expectations

As well as the processes of positive listings and affirmations described above, here is another technique to try out.

Reframe

The 'Reframe' is a very powerful technique for removing negative feelings and the effects they have on the actions you take in order to achieve your goals. There are many 'Reframe' techniques; one of them deals specifically with negative self-talk:

- Bring to mind your negative self-talk and the feeling you often experience associated with it.
- Try noticing where the sound seems to come from and move it (from the head, to the elbow or big toe).
- Try making the voice quieter, or have a different tone. Making the voice say the same thing, but much quicker or much slower, or sounding like Donald Duck!
- Try creating another voice that gets the negative one to shut up.
- Once the negative feelings have gone, repeat the process several times.
- Practise regularly. Five minutes a day, once a day, for ten days or two weeks is a good start.

Lack of self-confidence

Lack of self-confidence is another inner obstacle that influences the achievement of our goals. All too often, we make our confidence contingent upon external events. It is as if we are saying 'I will be confident.when I win, when I do well, when I get praised by a colleague' etc. It is as if we believe that actions comes first, and then comes confidence. In fact, it is the other way round: our level of confidence determines our actions.

Solutions to lack of self-confidence

- Clearly define in your mind what confidence would be like.
- Write or talk through some positive affirmations (as above).
- Relax and creatively visualise a confident state.
- Watch how positive people behave in different situations.
- Keep a log book focusing on positive experiences (as above).

It may well be that at the end of the day, the goals we give ourselves are only partially and sometimes not achievable. This is not as important as the actual setting of goals. Meaning and purpose are added to our day-to-day lives in the process of thinking through and taking some action. Goals can be changed and adapted to new events and circumstances. Yet, even such goals give us direction.

People with purpose

This section looks at people who have purpose in their lives. Some are famous; some are not. But for them all, a sense of purpose and meaning in life is bound up with some form of direct action. Tenzim Chozom decided to give up her comfortable life-style in Canada to become a nun. Her primary purpose has always been to be happy; that hasn't changed but the way she goes about it certainly has:

> *I guess the purpose of my life is to have a good time . . . to be happy. Like when I first went to Nepal I had this conversation with a friend . . . we sat and we talked for about four hours. He was wondering why are you doing this, why are you going on this retreat course for a month – he was from Nepal so he was naturally Buddhist by birth and he had his own car business. And we talked about the whole thing and we just got right to the bottom of it and we both came to the same conclusion that basically the whole thing is just to be happy. I felt like by becoming a nun I would be able to realise what true happiness really is and what makes you really happy . . . and I think I've come to understand that . . . it's not about selfishness it's about giving, benefiting others, it's about some kind of goodness.*

Chozom, Tibetan Buddhist Nun

Tracey's life became more meaningful when she decided to agree to stand up in court and speak about what she had seen:

> *My life suddenly took on a purpose when I agreed to be a witness. Six kids set on this other kid walking to the bus stop. They crushed his head in and beat him to death with sticks. I said nothing for a long time. I didn't want to get involved. I was frightened of what would happen to me. It was horrible . . . I had to have witness protection and live in this grotty little place. One of the cops said to me 'you've got a conscience, dozens of people saw the murder and aren't saying nothing but you said you saw it. You're doing something about it.*

Tracey, 'Wall of Silence' documentary, ITV, 2004

For some people like Tracey, a sense of purpose comes from an intense sense of injustice at what is going on in the world. A sense of injustice that leads to action. Throughout history, people from all kinds of backgrounds have made life for themselves very difficult by challenging the way their societies worked.

Nelson Mandela (born 1918) has been a political activist for over 60 years. He has never wavered in his purpose for all people to be treated equally. Despite torture and imprisonment, he never answered racism with racism. These words ending his statement from the dock in the Rivonia Trial in 1964, demonstrate Mandela's strength of purpose. He was prepared, if necessary, to die for his ideal:

> *During my lifetime I have dedicated myself to this struggle of the African people. I have fought against white domination, and I have fought against black domination. I have cherished the ideal of a democratic and free society in which all persons live together in harmony and with equal opportunities. It is an ideal which I hope to live for and to achieve. But if needs be, it is an ideal for which I am prepared to die.*

Mandela, 2000: 438

Mandela accomplished his dream and lived to see equality amongst all the people of South Africa. But his sense of purpose did not leave him: now he is working to eradicate poverty from the whole world.

The main purpose of Mahatma Gandhi's (1869–1948) life was centred on the continent of India. Gandhi struggled for Indian independence from Britain, Hindu-Muslim unity, the removal of the untouchable caste system and the emancipation of women. Mahatma Gandhi insisted on non-violence in order to achieve his aims. His ideas on non-violence were based on Hindu religious grounds (Gangrade, 2001: 25). At first he called his form of non-violence 'passive resistance' (a term he disavowed in later years). The technique was simple: declare opposition to an unjust law such as restrictions on free movement, break the law by crossing a border illegally, and suffer the consequences of arrest, physical abuse and prison. Gandhi believed that by resisting in a calm and dignified way, he could change the minds and actions of his oppressors because they would be obliged to see that this was the right way to go about things. Gandhi named this concept of action satyagraha combining the Hindu words satya for 'truth' and graha for 'holding firmly' (www.pbs.org/uk/learn/infodocs/people/gandhi).

Mahatma Gandhi did not achieve all his goals in his lifetime but he influenced many people all over the world including the black American civil rights leader Martin Luther King. Today, Gandhi's goal of non-violent resistance continues in that his grandson Arun Gandhi has set up the Gandhi Institute for Non-Violence (www.gandhiinstitute.org):

Non-violence is the first article of my faith. It is also the last article of my creed.

Gandhi, 1922

As Gandhi demonstrated and as John Donne wrote some 400 years before Gandhi, 'no man is an island, entire of itself; every man is a piece of the continent' (Coffin, 2001: 23). We are all citizens of the world, belonging to a huge planet of billions of people who, somehow, are connected and influence each other. Take for example, a factory worker in the UK, he may have put together a mobile phone eventually bought by a person in Pakistan, or the cereal you had for breakfast could have been grown in Kenya. And so on.

At the same time as unconsciously influencing and being influenced by citizens of other countries we can, as citizens of this country and as human beings of the world, act in order to make a difference to the world around us.

Activity: young people

Positive Action: a series of six sessions to promote positive action

The number of sessions is determined by how many people are involved, the length of the session and how much is covered in each session.

Overall Aims: To consider the difference positive action can make.
To commit to making a difference.

1st session

Aim: To think about the effect of positive action on other people.
Preparation: Photocopy of the 'Four Situations' handout, flip chart, pens.
Method: Ask each small group to thought-storm ideas about what they can realistically do in each of the four situations on the handout. Alternatively select one situation for each group to think about.

In large group, talk about how each group's findings can make a difference – locally and globally. Ask the group what positive actions they would like to take in future that could have an effect on others. Write down possible actions on flip chart.

For example:

- The right to vote
- The right to say what I think
- Getting involved
- Joining a campaign
- Signing a petition
- Becoming a Samaritan
- Working to eliminate poverty

Discuss the following questions:
1. What kind of world have we inherited?
2. How does it work?
3. What kind of world do we want?
4. How can we make the world the way we want it?

Ask the group to find out for the next session what other young people in the UK are doing to make a difference to their local communities and to the wider world we live in. Suggestions for useful web-sites are in the resource list at the end of the book.

2nd Session

Aim:	To commit to making a difference.
Preparation:	Collect information from the internet (suggestions for useful websites are in the resource list) and/or collect brochures from a selection of voluntary organisations, pressure groups, charitable and political campaigns. Bring along flip chart from first session. Paper and pens.
Method:	Recap the last session and look again at the positive actions written on the flip chart. Discuss what the group have found out since the last session about other young people making a difference in the UK. Divide into small groups and give each group writing material and a selection from the information you/they have collected. Each group then decides on a new or existing project to get behind.

Questions to consider are: What is the purpose of the project? What are my personal aims? Do my personal aims fit the project? What sort of help does the project need? What sort of help do I want to give and what sort of help can I realistically give? Decide what information is missing and how to research for the next session.

3rd and 4th Sessions

Aim:	To prepare a 5–10 minute presentation.
Preparation:	Flip chart, pens, paper, over head projector, transparencies, lap-top, photocopy of The Four Questions Handout.
Method:	Return to groups with information gained since the last session. Give each group The Four Questions Handout and ask them to begin to prepare their presentation by thought-storming the answers to the four questions. Decide who is going to do which section and who is going to prepare the visual aids.

Advice: Most presentations work well if there is a beginning – say what you are going to say, a middle – say it, and an ending – say what you have said, for example:

The beginning: *Today we are going to talk to you for about five minutes. At the end there will be time for questions. We are going to tell you about the aims of the campaign, its impact on the community and the opportunities for the entire group getting involved.*

The middle: *Give the aims, the impact on the community and explain the reasons to get involved, and how to get involved.*

The end: *Now we've told you a little about the campaign, its aims and what impact it has on the community and why and how we can all get involved. Thank you for listening and as we said at the beginning, we now can take questions. Thank you.*

5th and 6th sessions

Aim: To present findings.
Preparation: As in previous sessions.
Method: Each group presents findings and answers questions from the entire group. Group comes together to decide on one or several of the projects to initiate and/or support.

The purpose of life beyond the present experience

Even when our every day life is purposeful, occasionally life can still seem pointless. The pointlessness intensifies at certain times when we are completely overcome by the haphazardness of life. One moment walking on the pavement down the street, for example, and the next moment run over by a bus! What is the sense in that? What is the purpose of it happening?

Questions like these may also arise at times of great sadness and joy: when a baby is born, when we fall in love, when a best friend dies. Times when we are overwhelmed by the depth of feeling we experience, when our words fail us and we desire a deeper understanding of what is going on around us. It is at these moments of great purpose that we often sense that life has some meaning beyond the present experience.

Scientific research into the nature of consciousness together with many of the world's religions understand that human nature can be perceived as having two aspects: the material and the spiritual. The spiritual side of human nature – in many religious traditions referred to as the soul – is that part of our being that continually seeks to understand more about ourselves and other people, that wants to love and be loved, that is affected by the beauty of the physical world around us and believes in the power of doing good:

I think there are so many questions to ask that lead to more and more questions. Ultimately to perhaps the most challenging of all questions: what is the purpose of my existence? Because for the first time there is introduced into the questioning a sense of 'activity'. Before, the questions were all passive . . . things happened; I was born; why? I came from somewhere; where? I am; who? Now, suddenly, there is introduced this sense of 'doing'; of purpose. What is the purpose of my existence? Perhaps of all the deep questions this is the one that makes me most hopeful that I can do something to make a difference.

Joel

The 20th century theologian Emil Brunner said, 'What oxygen is to the lungs, such is hope to the meaning of life'. Without hope, life can become virtually meaningless. But let's make a distinction here between hope and wishes, wants and dreams. Deep down, hope is not about relying on horoscopes, the lottery or dreaming of fame and fortune.

Meaningful hope goes much deeper and actually stirs us to action. Ultimately, it is not just about us, but about our relationships and the impact we have on those around us. Former President of the Czech Republic, Vaclav Havel wrote 'Hope . . . is not the same as joy that things are going well, or willingness to invest in enterprises that are obviously headed for success, but rather an ability to work for something because it makes sense, not just because it stands a chance to succeed. It is this hope, above all, which gives us the strength to live and continually to try new things, even in conditions that seem as hopeless as ours do, here and now'.

This deep hope can be described as a kind of faith: a sense of trust and conviction that gives a continuing purpose to life. This kind of deep hope can also be described as spirituality: a sense of something more important than ourselves and a sense that we can make a difference to the people and the environment around us.

It is a very challenging kind of spirituality because it involves trying something that may not work. It involves change and the realisation that we do not have all the answers.

The Four Situations Handout

1. Being involved in local planning (e.g. youth centre/services)
Put yourself in the position of living in a run-down small town where there is nothing to do except hang around with your mates on the street.
What can you do about it?

2. Conserving the environment
Put yourself in your grandparent's shoes in 2050. The earth is filled up with rubbish, the cities are flooding and the ozone layer is rapidly disappearing.
What can you do about it?

3. Raising money for a third world water project
Put yourself in the position of having to walk five miles each way to get drinking water.
What can you do about it?

4. Giving time to older people
Put yourself in the position of an older person who is stuck at home all day.
What can you do about it?

The Four Questions Handout

1. What is my basic message?

2. What is my purpose?
   (to sell, entertain, interest, inspire action, persuade, inform, teach, answer questions, show results, etc.)

3. Who is my audience?

4. What do they expect to hear?

Chapter 3

Am I Really Alone?

Most people know what it feels like to be alone but loneliness means different things to different people. This chapter looks beneath the many social issues that can cause loneliness. It distinguishes between loneliness, isolation and being alone and at the same time acknowledges the inter-connectedness of these feelings. Throughout the chapter there are personal statements from young people, activities and ideas for coping with loneliness. At the end of the chapter there is advice on how to set up a reflection group designed to help colleagues and young people achieve inner peace and calm. The overriding message is that being alone can be a positive experience; part of the journey leading to growing self-knowledge, self-acceptance and awareness of an inner life.

Loneliness

We often hear comments like: 'I'm the only one who doesn't get it', 'No-one likes me', 'I haven't got any friends'. Usually this kind of loneliness is temporary but in some cases, it is more profound and can lead to extreme feelings of isolation.

Adolescence is often the time when people feel intensely passionate about their friends. Loneliness can take the form of missing and wanting to be with a special person. A real sense of loss. Or loneliness can be not having anyone to miss! Badly wanting to be with a particular person or have a particular person to be with, is sometimes felt most acutely when surrounded by a crowd of people.

Loneliness may also be the result of imaginary or real perception about the situation: really looking or sounding different or imagining you look or sound different from everyone else; thinking you don't have the 'right' dialect or fashion accessories:

> I think loneliness is often a 'why me' sort of thing as opposed to 'what am I doing?' It's more of why is it me that's in this difficult situation or why don't I have more friends or why did I have that problem in my relationship or why am I not the best at this? A sense of being held back in my own mind by my lack of achievement, by my lack of confidence in myself.
>
> Jade

Living at home

Dramatic emotional, physical and intellectual transitions that can occur in adolescence may result in disagreeing with family or peer group values (Wheal, 1999: 26). A clash of values and attitudes can temporarily and sometimes permanently create a sense of being an outsider within the family group. Jossi prefers to stay home on his own because he doesn't agree with the way his family do things:

> They always go to church Sunday mornings and then they go to the pub and then they go shopping.. I don't go with them anymore . . . they come back home and then have a go at me for not going but I think it's so hypocritical . . . one minute they're praying, the next minute they're shopping . . . it gets a bit lonely at times but I'd rather stay at home.
>
> Jossi

David is lonely at home because he does not want to bring friends home because he is embarrassed by the way his parents behave:

> *I never brought friends home 'cos my mum and dad used to fight . . . he'd come home drunk and he'd sometimes hit her. You never knew when it would happen. I just remember her standing there screaming.*

David

Leaving home

Ideally leaving home is a gradual process but sometimes the decision to leave is sudden or forced. Many young people leave home after a row, spend some time with a relation or friend and return home. A few have no-one to talk to and no place to stay. They may travel away from their hometown, often to a big city where they cannot be easily found:

> *I've just turned 17 and I left home earlier this year. I started doing sex work because of this man I met. Easy money but I've got no one to speak to, I just feel really lonely and locked up.*

Mark

Sexuality

Uncertainty over sexual identity is sometimes a cause of loneliness. Adolescents generally like to conform with their peers, so discovering that one is different can be most uncomfortable. Gay young people may feel that they do not fit in with others in their age group. Some may find it difficult to go to school or join in school activities such as team sports. Others such as high academic achievers may find solace in studying hard. Many find themselves shying away from heterosexual socialisation such as the 'school disco' or even the canteen:

> *I thought I was 'different' from a very young age (7 or 8) but I know that I have to pretend to 'fit in' and act 'normal' if I want my family to accept me. I became a bit of a rebel and the joker at school as a way of feeling part of a group, and it was also a great distraction from what was really going on inside . . . now I feel lonely and confused and I'm not sure that something's not wrong with me or it's just me being stupid.*

Pardeep

Here is an activity that aims to find ways to cope with loneliness. Be aware that you might be stirring up real issues that affect the participants. So you need to be prepared to talk about these issues afterwards and if it turns out to be a problem that the young person wants to talk about in more depth, you may need to refer to a counselling service.

Activity: young people

Dear problem page, I'm on my own

Aim: To create strategies to cope with loneliness.
Preparation: Photocopy handout (page 39).
Method: Distribute handout to pairs.
             Ask each pair to discuss and suggest ways of coping with the situation.
             In group, listen to the different ways and discuss. It may be useful to ask these questions:

1. Can time make a difference to being lonely?
2. How can other people help?
3. How many points of view can there be on this particular problem?

Isolation

Feeling isolated is a profound sense of being on your own, being apart from others. The word 'isolation' carries with it the idea of unwelcome or imposed solitude for long periods of time, such as being in prison or in an isolation ward. We may suffer isolation because of circumstances created by others over which we have no control. For example:

Forced exile

Young people may be forced to leave their own country when they are experiencing, or are threatened by persecution. Many refugees and asylum seekers find themselves in temporary accommodation having to adjust to a new climate and culture:

> *I felt desperate when I first arrived here. No-one understood what I was saying, I was cold and uncomfortable . . . I think the most difficult thing now is having to cook and eat all by myself, I don't think I have ever eaten alone before. And even if I have learnt how to prepare basic meals I am a very bad cook and then you have to eat it by yourself.*
>
> Michael in 'Wheal', 2002: 134

Enforced change of peer group

During adolescence identifying with a peer group is important. Changing school, college or job leads to an enforced change of peer group. All peer groups have common characteristics such as norms of behaviour, music and clothes preferences and a pecking order. Often in order to be accepted as one of the 'crowd', it is necessary to observe the group culture. A lack of observance of the group culture may lead to bullying, harassment and discrimination (Clifton and Serdar, 2000: 20).

> *I miss my mates so much. I hate being here. I think the new crowd are laughing at me behind my back. I'm not sure why . . . I just don't think it's the way I dress . . . my trainers or my hair or both.*
>
> Jay

Leaving care

Young people leaving care may face the reality that they have to cope on their own. In some cases, they are not prepared and feel extremely isolated:

> *I felt completely isolated . . . I didn't know the area, I didn't do my research. I felt pressured to have the flat now. My neighbours . . . I'm in fear of my safety. I wish that I'd refused it. Young people shouldn't be pushed into a flat.*
>
> Chantal

Special needs and disabilities

Learning, emotional or behavioural difficulties, sight and hearing impairment and wheelchair users are among the many special needs and disabilities that may result in isolation (Barnes, 2002: 80–3).

I live in the world of silence. I am surrounded by hearing people who I don't understand. I always feel isolated near them. They hear music and they go to the cinema. And me? I always feel bored at home. I sit and sit.

Marek

Being Alone

Being alone as opposed to being lonely or isolated can be a positive experience. To be alone, is to be free. No-one else is in control and there is no need to control others. It is a time to relax and just 'be' in contrast to a time to 'do'. It is an opportunity to evaluate what is going on in life as opposed to responding without thought to what is happening. In a curious way, when we are alone we can be pro-active rather than passive:

I like being alone surrounded by people I don't know. It's exciting, anything can happen. Yesterday I was on the train and it was delayed because of leaves on the lines and the two people next to me started to talk and laugh and I joined in.

Joanna

Aloneness is part of our development from babies to children and on to adolescence and adulthood. When we are young we derive our ideas about ourselves from parents and carers. As we grow older, our identity and opinions are often confirmed and supported by friends rather than family.

The French psychologist Jean Piaget (1896–1980) wrote about the parent-child conflict being part of the process of becoming an adult during the teenage years. Through conflict, we develop autonomy and start making choices for ourselves. Piaget's theory stresses that in adolescence, individuals experience a period of individuation – a time when we realise our separate existence, a time that we realise we are alone and begin to enjoy our independence. When we are truly mature we may still take advice from friends and family but ultimately our choices are made from our own assessment of the situation. And for that, we need more – not less – time alone (Fontana, 1992: 48–50).

Being alone makes us aware of ourselves as distinct from other people. We have the chance to consider who we are, what we are doing and what we want. We have time to note our unique differences from every other human being. Often our identities become wrapped up in job, school, family, television programmes and films: in fact, a lot that is external. This is not to say these things are not important and enriching but sometimes to be alone is to put ourselves into a different context. One in which we don't have to worry about paying bills, answering e-mails and sending text messages. A context in which we can consider what is really important in our lives. For a while, we have a chance to think carefully and to live in the moment of being. If we are alone, we are with ourselves.

In a way, a person is always alone. There's an old cliché that sums it up – 'we come into this world on our own and we go out on our own!' What happens in between involves a lot of other human beings. The degree to which we are involved with other people varies a lot. The philosopher and poet, Kahil Gibran points out that an individual, however much in love with another, is still alone. In his poem 'The Prophet', he suggests that the essence of a human being – the unique inside part that is different from everyone else is absolutely alone and that being alone is part of the human condition (Gibran, 1994: 16). Every human being is able to use 'aloneness'. It can help us to understand ourselves and other people better. Being alone can also give us a sense of going beyond ourselves. A sense of wonder about the world. A sense that there is more to life than the material world.

> Give yourself a mind break
> Give yourself a heart break
> Get away from it all
> Take time to be yourself
> Take time to find yourself

There may be very practical reasons to get away from everybody else and from everyday distractions. If you don't want interruptions, using the local library to write or playing music in the garden shed is a good idea! But at the same time, either consciously or unconsciously, something else is happening. To enable that story or music to evolve often involves reaching deep within and/or far outside ourselves. Creativity is a mixture of the mental and the emotional; the external and the internal; the physical and the spiritual. And being alone can be part of that creativity.

> **Centre for Spirituality**
> Retreats, quiet days, personal reflection.
> We can offer you space, quiet, some time to reflect in peace away from your usual daily life.
> Spend a day or more in contemplation.
> We are able to provide spiritual guidance during your time here if you wish, and can cater for individuals and groups in simple, comfortable surroundings.

Many people – both secular and religious – realise the value of 'taking time out'. Here Daniel describes his experience in retreat.

> *I did this short retreat . . . just a nine day one. It was a lot of sitting down and walking and doing yoga. You'd get up quite early in the morning and do an hour's meditation and have a cup of tea. There was just this sense that you were trying to integrate thoughtfulness and reflection into the everyday. So if you were sweeping the yard or cleaning the bathroom or whatever you were doing, you were doing it thoughtfully. And the urge to talk sort of was there but it was quite nice not to have to talk all the time. In fact it kind of relieved you of this sense of entertaining and having to constantly engage. In a way what I found was it was a more profound sort of level of engagement when you actually have to think about your life a little bit and also a sense of calm that came.*
>
> Daniel

Lee describes the positive aspects of solitude:

> *I didn't feel isolated or lonely, I felt alone but comfortably alone in a positive sense . . . in the sense that I don't often get the chance to just sit, to just be somewhere . . . there was a sense of peace about it. A chance to look at yourself and feel comfortable with some things and reflect upon who you are and what you are doing and also to try and see where you're at outside the context of your own external life.*
>
> Lee

Meditation

Meditation is a positive way of coping with loneliness and isolation. It is a way of making a fresh start and seeing ourselves with new insight and it offers an opportunity to find out who we are and where we are going. Meditation is listening to ourselves and the thoughts that we don't know we have! Nearly all spiritual traditions have at their base meditation and contemplative practices. In recent years many of these techniques have also been recommended as a basis for good health.

The traditional Buddhist style of meditation aims to develop consciousness, awaken compassion and concentrate the mind through focusing on the act of breathing. By focusing on the breath or one thought or one object rather than on a whole host of things, the mental chatter dies down. We can become aware of the smallness of whatever it is that might have been bothering us compared to the big outside world. And we can gradually become ever more open and responsive to the inner voice within us:

> *There's a lot of trust just to sit in a room with your eyes closed and kind of focus on the breath or visualisation. I found it much easier to do with a group of people.you need to do it where there is a supportive environment, where there are people where you can talk to and discuss things and you feel safe and secure . . . what I got out of it . . . basic relaxation, sense of calming the mind a bit, a sense of community, a sense of doing something a bit different.*
>
> Daniel

The meditation exercise suggested here is a very basic technique and there is certainly no idea of altering states of consciousness. Nevertheless, during this practice or some time later, disturbing issues may arise. Make sure you have the time to listen. If necessary, be prepared to contact an appropriate professional who is able to deal with the issues you have unearthed. If you are not familiar with meditation, try out the techniques before introducing them to other people.

Meditation exercise

- Prepare your space. You can meditate standing up or sitting down, whichever you find most comfortable. However, if you're feeling tired, it's probably best not to lie down or you may run the risk of falling asleep!

- Focus on a spot or an object in the room – a mark on the ceiling, a clock or a picture. Stare at it intently and gradually allow yourself to become aware of everything that is around your chosen spot or object.

- After a couple of minutes, you will begin to feel a sense of relaxation. At this point, close your eyes.

- Begin to concentrate on your breathing. Avoid sharp intakes of breath. Breathe in a little through the nose. Hold the breath and then release it through the mouth. Think of a bottle that fills up from the bottom not the top. That is what you are doing when you breathe deeply from your abdomen. When you breathe from the upper chest, air presses on the heart, raises the blood pressure and increases the feelings of stress. However, breathing from the abdomen means that this air presses down on the abdomen, massaging the intestine and alleviating tension.

- The final stage of your meditation need last no longer than two minutes or can go on for as long as you feel you need. How you approach it depends on the type of person you are. If you are someone who prefers visual stimuli, use your imagination to create a mental picture of something that you find particularly calming. The candle flame is a classic image used in meditation, but any image that relaxes you can be used – a beach, a smiling baby, a waterfall. If you are a more auditory person, try beginning to count in time with your breathing. Counting on the exhalations only, count from one to ten. When you reach ten, begin at one again.

- When you have completed your meditation, gradually open your eyes and look around you. You will probably feel relaxed and rejuvenated, because the mental process clears the clutter from your mind and enables you to take a fresh look at everything.

Setting up a reflection group

Simple meditation techniques are easy to start but hard to maintain. Consider establishing a reflection group for colleagues or the young people you work with. A reflection group provides an opportunity for a 'tranquillity zone' – a space with soft furnishing, music, candles and flowers and for a 'discovery zone' – a different area in which to offer some of the activities described in this chapter and elsewhere in the book.

Schedule sessions on a regular basis or hold daily meetings within the context of a residential weekend or holiday. As well as well as formal meditation techniques, possible uses for the 'tranquillity zone' are sketching in pictures or words, journaling observations of feelings and reflections, quiet thought and prayer.

Stop and Think: you/colleagues

What is prayer? What is private prayer? What is communal prayer? Is private prayer different from communal prayer? Why?

Whether you are used to praying or not, the subject of meditation and prayer is one that enables you to share values with people from both a non-faith and faith perspective. Here are two activities for people of all backgrounds .

Activity: colleagues/young people

Wishing and Praying

Aim: To consider the difference between wishing and praying.
Preparation: Photocopy of the 'Four Statements' handout.
Method: Divide into pairs or small groups to consider the Four Statements and the questions beneath the statements on the handout.
                  Return to large group to pool ideas. Discuss the differences between wishing and praying. Consider the difference between desperately wanting to do something well and prayer. How does wishing and praying help to improve the world? How can wishing and praying help to improve the individual? Ask group to think about what they would say in a wish or a prayer. Nobody has to say aloud: it maybe something to think about during the meditation exercise. You can also invite participants to write down their own prayers/wishes.

Activity: colleagues/young people

Other People at Prayer

Aim: To find out how other people pray.

Preparation: Photocopy 'Personal Statements About Prayer' handout.

Method: In pairs or small groups discuss each personal statement. What does each statement say about prayer? What are the strengths of each type of prayer? How do you relate to the statement? How do your ideas differ from the statement?

In large group, pool ideas emphasising the diverse range of experience of prayer. If there are people from faith groups present ask them to share their experiences of prayer. For example, a Muslim could demonstrate and explain the prayer position for facing Mecca, a Hindu could talk about why they pray at a small shrine in the home and a Jewish person could describe the Sabbath service in the synagogue. If everyone is from the same or different faith backgrounds, discuss whether people get the same out of prayer regardless of faith and talk about the different ways prayer is carried out within one faith. If the majority of people in the group have a non-faith perspective, ask them to consider the difference between desperately wanting to do well at something and prayer.

Problem Page Handout

If you had to reply, what would you say?

Dear,
I broke up with Jack last week. We'd been going together for ages. I just can't stop crying. I've got like a terrible pain inside. I've got no-one to talk to and I feel so lonely. What can I do to feel better?

Dear,
I love my mum but I've always found it easier to talk to my aunt. I go round there a lot, especially when I've had a row at home. Yesterday when I was round there, she told me she's changing job and moving away – a long way away. She says she'll phone but it won't be the same. I'll be really lonely without her. What should I do?

Dear,
I really like Aisha and I've been going out with her quite a while. When I'm with her we talk quite a lot. But when we meet her friends down the pub, she keeps on talking to them and ignores me. It makes me feel so alone and then I get a really angry feeling inside. I really want to hit out and dump her. Do you think I should?

Dear,
My parents seem to have rows all the time. They both expect me to take their side. I've heard them talking about divorce. It's been going on a while. I can't talk about it because no one else knows. I feel so on my own. What should I do for the best?

Dear,
I'm being bullied at school. I feel lonely. I don't fit in. I don't understand why. Help?

Dear,
My girl-friend's pregnant but she doesn't want to have the baby. She says if she's stuck at home with a baby, she'll miss all her friends and be lonely. I want her to have the baby. Am I right?

Dear,
I think I'm very overweight so I don't have any friends. Nobody invites me out at the weekends. What should I do?

The Four Statements Handout – Wishing and Praying

I wish I had more time with my mum.

Amir

1. What would you call a thought like this if God's name is included?
2. What would you call it if God's name is not included?
3. Does a thought only become a prayer when God's name is included?

I find personal prayer very difficult. The idea that God has nothing better to do than to listen to me moaning about my boyfriend Nick is just too ridiculous. But when the chips are down, I do it. The other night at one o'clock in the morning I lay awake having a panic attack. Nick was out with his mates and I was sure something awful had happened to him. What did I do? I prayed like mad of course.

Ciska

1. Does Ciska think that prayer will help?
2. Is this a prayer?
3. If you think it is, what makes it a prayer?
4. If not, what is it?

Thank you God for giving me such a wonderful brother, who was like a father to me. He was the kindest, sweetest person I ever knew. Having neither father nor mother, he made my life liveable and tried to fill the emptiness with good times. Please thank him for all the good he did for me. I am so lonely because I have missed him terribly since he departed some five years ago.

Don

1. Is this a prayer?
2. Why?
3. If yes, what kind of prayer is it?
4. Will this help Don to be less lonely?
5. If so, how?

Dear God, Mesma's in a mess. She can't get her act together. One minute she's decided what she's going to do. Then the next minute she told me she definitely didn't want to do that. I don't know what is going to happen if she doesn't sort it out soon. Please see to it God.

Kira

1. Can Kira expect an answer?
2. Can prayer be said on behalf of someone else?
3. Do you think the prayer is likely to be answered if Mesma does not believe in prayer?

'Personal Statements About Prayer' Handout

We go into the mosque and we stand next to each other, all facing Mecca. We wait for the Imam to begin. We raise our hands to our shoulders and say 'Allah Akbar' . . . God is Great which signifies the beginning of prayer. Then we bend and put our hands on our knees . . . the Ruku position and then we rise and stand upright before going into the bow . . . the Sujood position where our noses and foreheads touch the ground. I guess it is at that point that you feel closest to God because we would never bow in that fashion to anyone else.

Anisa

I like to pray because it allows me time to take stock of the things that have happened in my day, it's a relief from worry and a time to be thankful. I just close the door and as long as it's fairly quiet I pray.

Manual

I am quite religious and in the mornings I do the Mool Mantra which is the first prayer in our religion and then I say my own personal prayer of what I want in the day. It's not only about religious stuff, I also ask God to help me . . . like if I'm finding something hard. I feel I have quite a close relationship with God. I go every Sunday to a Punjabi class and I know quite a lot about Sikhism. Knowing more about Sikhism makes me feel closer to God but I think in the main it's the meditation.We call God Wahiguru which basically means wonderful teacher . . . I think that by saying that for five, ten minutes helps you get to God. I try to visualise God and I think that after you pray quite a lot and meditate a lot you probably do get an image of God. I haven't got there yet.

Sahib

I find my daily practice gives me a positive approach, opens my heart and helps me to be more accepting of myself and others. I am less fearful, more joyful and content. I get up at 5.45am to first of all do prostrations bowing before my altar to the teachings of the Buddha and my own potential for enlightenment (of Buddhahood). I then sit in the half lotus position which means sitting with my back straight with my legs crossed with one open palm of my hand resting on the other and my thumbs joined for half an hour saying my prayers and mantras. This leads into a simple meditation practice which focuses my mind on the present moment.

At the end of the day I again do prayers and sit in meditation dedicating any small accomplishments of the day for the happiness of all beings. I believe that prayer and meditation with love and compassion can really touch hearts and minds and send out positive energy to the world.

Sue

Prayer for me is two-fold . . . the private and the communal. I enjoy the communal . . . being in the synagogue amongst lots of people that I know, hearing the beautiful ancient melodies and sometimes joining in the singing, sometimes daydreaming and sometimes concentrating on the meaning of the prayers and just thanking God for everything I have going for me. That's really the easy bit. When it comes to personal prayer, I find it much more difficult. When I'm not surrounded by other people's fervour, I'm doubtful whether there's any point to prayer. The only time, I feel a real surge to pray is when I'm overwhelmed by an extreme condition . . . I'm worried to death or I'm ecstatically happy about something. It seems to me that the only way I'll ever change that is if I get into regular prayer . . . I'd have to do it so it becomes a habit and then maybe it would be easier but then would it just be easier because it was a habit and not because it is true . . . I really don't know.

Ben

Chapter 4

Why do Bad Things Happen?

Amongst all the big questions about life, perhaps the most difficult is why do bad things happen. On an individual level, why does one person enjoy an apparently happy and successful life whilst another experiences bad times. And on a global scale, why do catastrophes such as earthquakes and floods kill thousands of people?

This chapter considers what can go wrong and how we respond when things go wrong. It looks briefly at what the psychologist Sigmund Freud and what the moral philosophers John Hick and Richard Swinburne have to say. There is also an outline of the views of six faith communities. Throughout young people express their views. The chapter concludes with questions to think about and strategies for coping when things go wrong. The premise being that the bad things that happen can become part of the search for meaning – the search for the answer to 'Who Am I?'

What can go wrong?

Lots of different things can go wrong in our lives and in the lives of the young people that we work with. Some of them, although fairly trivial, are extremely important at the time. For example, when something goes wrong with our appearance, the image we have of ourselves can alter. We may temporarily lose part of our identity that gives us confidence and self-esteem:

> When I had my hair coloured and it turned out all wrong I was devastated. I didn't go out for days . . . I just sat in front of the telly . . . I felt like there was no point to anything . . . I just looked so awful.
>
> Kelly

Some things that go wrong persist over a long period of time: we may not even remember a time when life was any different:

> My dad's an alcoholic. I'm used to him coming in drunk. I can't go to sleep until I know he's gone to bed and know he won't start hitting mum. I can't see how it'll change.
>
> Terry

Yet for most of us life is not so chaotic. We take, in the main, our lives for granted and there are few highs and lows. Sometimes we are even bored with the banal routine of everyday life. But then suddenly something goes wrong. Something unexpectedly happens that turns everything upside down. It may be a situation that undermines our sense of security like a sibling, whom we have relied upon, suddenly leaves home . . . a parent loses their job . . . a close friend dies.

> I never expected it to work out like this . . . my friend wasn't feeling very well. At first they thought it was nerves but it didn't get better. She saw loads of doctors, she got really upset and then she was told it was leukaemia.
>
> Kumba

How do we respond when things go wrong?

At first, when something bad unexpectedly happens, we can be confused and disorientated. Not getting into the football team, failing exams or breaking up with a partner means an unsettling change in how we expect life to be:

> *When Michelle dumped me I was really angry. I didn't know what I'd done wrong. She made me feel like a waste of space . . . we'd been together for ages . . . and I thought it was going to stay like that.*
>
> Sean

Some people respond to an on-going difficult situation by simply pretending everything's alright:

> *Everything will be OK. I'll stop drinking so much and doing drugs. I'll start to do my work and pass my exams . . . everything's fine.*
>
> Fatmata

Sometimes, we are just getting over one difficulty when something else happens. With each ensuing problem our ability to cope lessens. And we may respond by taking a decision that we really need help to make:

> *My father had just died and we moved house about the same time. It was a huge upheaval. Then I got pregnant and practically immediately I had an abortion. I didn't talk to anyone, I didn't see a counsellor, and I just went and did it. Looking back on it, I can see I wasn't in a fit state to take such a decision and I wish I'd at least spoken to someone who had been through what I was going through . . . someone who'd had to make the choice that I felt I had to make.*
>
> Channah

'It's not fair' may well be the initial response to illness and accidents that strike at random:

> *The saddest time of my life was when my mum died – she was so young – I felt robbed really . . . I felt it was unfair and at times I felt jealous of people who still have their mums. Why me? What had I done to deserve that to happen to me . . . it just wasn't fair.*
>
> Concey

Following on from the reaction of 'it's not fair', comes the 'why did it go wrong, why did it happen to me, who's to blame' syndrome. In our minds, there may be many reasons why we think things have gone wrong. We might blame ourselves or blame other people, or we may think of the bad thing that's happened as a random event that is no-body's fault or we may blame God.

Blaming ourselves

Sometimes when things go wrong, we blame ourselves although we are not necessarily to blame. For example, children of divorced parents may blame themselves for the break-up of the marriage. Perhaps, a distinction needs to be made here between 'concern' and 'blame'. It may be our concern that our parents are divorced but we are not to blame; it is not our fault:

> *My parents divorced three years ago and I still think maybe it could be different. Maybe if I hadn't sided with mum all the time, dad would have stayed. Maybe, I should have handled it differently.*
>
> Jo

Other times we think bad things happen because we did something wrong in the past and we are now being punished:

> *I know why this has happened to me. Once I'd left home, I never bothered getting in touch. For years I didn't call her and tell her that I was alright. Now it's too late and it's all my fault.*

Vella

The idea of punishment is an expression of the notion of common justice that insists if you've done something wrong you pay for it. Perhaps a combination of upbringing, conscience and tribal instinct produces this feeling of 'payback' deep inside us. The desire for revenge has always been around. And when bad things happen sometimes we take revenge on ourselves.

According to the psychologist Sigmund Freud (1856–1939) our earliest childhood memories may well be of when we misbehaved and were threatened with punishment. Freud put forward the theory that punishment is a sign to the child of loss of love and bound to be feared on its own account. As we get older, Freud suggests that we punish ourselves, even if we were not severely punished as children. In Freud's view it is all to do with what is going on in the mind where there are three levels of identity: the id or unconscious mind with which a baby is born, the ego or preconscious mind that develops around the end of the first year of life and the super-ego or conscious mind that develops around the age of six. The super-ego is the agency in the ego that judges and punishes the ego in the same way as the parent/carer used to do. So the super-ego monitors what we do and say and judges and punishes.

Freud considers the super-ego to be the origin of conscience. He asserts that the beginning of the moral sense of guilt is the tension between the ego and the super-ego.

This is where psychology and theology somewhat overlap. Concepts of good and bad and reward and punishment are important aspects of religious thinking. Many religions depict God as a law giver – giving human beings codes of conduct. This tends to equate God with the parent figure or super-ego inside our minds. When we know we have done something wrong, we expect to be punished. Just as ordinary parents can impose punishments so we imagine that God – 'the parent in the sky' – is punishing us by making things go wrong in our lives:

> *I must have done something wrong when I was a kid to deserve this because otherwise I can't understand why I developed breast cancer in my twenties. It's just not fair. I do lots of good things – I work hard, I give money to charity, I'm a good mum and I don't break the law. Why me? Why is this happening to me when I'm basically a good person?*

Carol

Carol had high expectations that her life would run smoothly because she has worked hard all her life and behaves well towards others. From birth, we are influenced by the work ethic that suggests that if we try hard and behave well, we will do well. We are told when little that if we do such and such a thing we will be rewarded. The reward may be expressed as the pleasure our parents or carers show us or something more tangible like buying a toy. As we get older, parents and carers may say that if you work hard, you'll get good grades.

High achievement in financial terms is valued in our society. Hard work is considered part of that model. It is a social class phenomenon with the middle classes often more aspirational in terms of trying to build better lives. Better lives are those that are considered to be full of achievement. The ultimate 'better' life is fame and celebrity. The drive to achieve more and more is justified by the results. Our expectations often preclude the difficulties that can stand in the way of those achievements.

We – the people who work with young people – unwittingly reinforce these attitudes every time we tell a young person to work harder so they'll have a better life because they'll get a better job, etc. When this does not materialise and/or something unexpectedly goes wrong; they may well be confused and look for someone to blame.

Blaming others

Have you ever caught yourself thinking 'it's X's fault I haven't got my papers . . . they must have moved them' and then five minutes later you find them under a pile of your own papers?

And more seriously, when lots of important things are going wrong, have you noticed how easy it is to blame someone else? Often done to the exclusion of accepting any degree of responsibility ourselves:

> *When I stormed out, I thought it was all their fault. They made more fuss of my brother, he was always the one who did everything right. They paid out things for him that they didn't do for me. Now I can see that it wasn't all one way. I did some pretty nasty things to them but at the time, I just wanted someone else to blame for lots of things that were going wrong for me.*
>
> Nazma

There are situations where two people have different opinions on who is to blame:

> *Della thinks it's Barny's fault that he gets bullied all the time. She says Barny should stand up for himself. I don't see it like that. I think the kids who bully him are to blame.*
>
> Linda

Blaming no-one

We may think that it is really nobody's fault when something bad happens. Some people just shrug their shoulders and get on with it with either a pessimistic attitude that 'life's bad, bad things happen, it's the nature of the world' or an optimistic attitude that 'so what, it could be far worse, life can only improve'.

Fatalism is the term for the belief that all events are determined to happen the way they do in fact happen no matter what we do to try to avoid them. This concept is both a theological and philosophical one. In terms of some theologies, all that the individual is and becomes is caused by God's power operating in conjunction with God's will. Nothing that the individual does will alter that fixed plan. Only that which God has ordained to happen happens and that which happens is that which God has ordained to happen (Angeles, 1992: 111).

In terms of some philosophies, a person is a product of pre-deterministic forces operating in the universe. An individual cannot in any way direct his or her behaviour or destiny, or that of history. No one can help being what he or she is and acting as he or she does (Angeles, 1992: 110).

Moral philosophers Hick and Swinburne divide the bad things that happen into two categories: Natural and moral faults both called 'evils'. This does not mean 'wickedness' in the way a tabloid headline might. It's more to do with ideas about the conditions we live in. The idea that the world is not perfect and nor are we so things are bound to go wrong from time to time.

Types of evil

Natural evil

Natural evil is the evil that originates independently of human actions, in disease, in bacilli, in earthquakes, storms, droughts, tornados etc.
John Hick, 1968

Moral evil

Moral evil I understand as including all evil caused deliberately by humans doing what they ought not to do, and also the evil constituted by deliberate actions or negligent failure.
Richard Swinburne, 1996

Keenan, 2004: 1

Natural evil is the result of usual or unusual natural occurrences. For example, the South Asian tsunami at the end of 2004 destroyed villages and crops, made thousands homeless and over 300,000 people lost their lives:

> *My grandchildren are crying all the time because they have lost their mother. There are gangs around that want to take young children away. We have lost our home, we need shelter, water and food . . . I must take care of them. They need food, water and shelter.*
>
> Apeelamma

Moral evil is the result of deliberate human action. When we look at the history of human behaviour over thousands of years it is clear that many individuals have been responsible for inflicting a great deal of pain and suffering on others. For example, Hitler's Germany engineered the killing of millions of people, including Jews, homosexuals and gypsies:

> *We were waiting in lines as names were being read out. There was a young dark-haired woman in front of me who had a knapsack on her back. A soldier was walking slowly along the line of people; casually glancing at us every now and then. He paused near us. He came closer to the young woman and peered at her. Suddenly, detecting some slight movement in her knapsack, he began to hit her with his truncheon. She screamed and pleaded with him, trying to avoid his blows and begging him not to kill her baby. Again and again, I heard the sickening thud of his truncheon amid her shrieks. But all her pleas were useless. I will never forget the gloating look of satisfaction on his face as he killed that child. His grinning face has haunted me all my life.*
>
> Hela

Blaming God

Once we bring God into the 'why have things gone wrong' equation, we are faced with an enormous dilemma. If God is so good and so powerful, how come bad things happen? Is God to blame for this? Or does there exist a malevolent power separate from the good God that is determined to destroy goodness and happiness?

There are times when everything appears so appalling that it seems there must be some major force of evil that delights in ruining our world and us. Or is it the evil force that is part of our human nature? One of the oldest responses to the question of evil show the gods destroying the whole human race because of what it has done wrong, as in the story of the flood in ancient Babylonian literature and in the Biblical book of Genesis, Chapters 6–8.

All religions take the bad things that individuals do seriously. The problem is agreeing on what's bad! What one branch within one religion may think is outrageous, another branch of the same religion may think is reasonable. Nevertheless, all religions offer ways to resist doing wrong. Many religious traditions seem to strike pre-emptively to remind us of the consequences of our actions.

Here is a brief guide to some of the ways that Buddhism, Christianity, Hinduism, Islam, Judaism and Sikhism account for the bad things that happen. Remember that within each faith tradition there are many different doctrines. Also it is noteworthy that the personal statements included here do not necessarily represent the traditional teachings of the faith tradition.

 Buddhism

According to Buddhism bad things happen if we try to cling on to something stable, something that is going to endure in this world where nothing is permanent. This includes clinging on to positive or negative feelings as well as to possessions. The teaching of the Buddha, the founder of Buddhism, points to a way to loosen and eventually break the bond of attachment to this world, or even to our 'selves'. It may take many lifetimes to achieve but at that time suffering will end and we will realise that there is nothing permanent or ever lasting to be attached to:

> *I think if I suffer now it is because in a previous life there was an ignorant action . . . either anger or killing . . . we all need so much and we don't see that we are all the same, we are all trying to find happiness and we don't understand that we're not the centres of the universe. We've got to free ourselves from wanting so much . . . free ourselves from attachment . . . from desire . . . It's not because we're bad or that it is our fault . . . it's just like a computer misprogramming . . . it's just a tweak of the mind that doesn't see clearly and that's where great compassion can be born . . . just understanding that misguided actions are so unnecessary.*
>
> Tenzin Chozom

The Four Noble Truths lie at the root of Buddhism, and these truths analyse the dukkha, the suffering that Tenzin Chozom is talking about. The first truth is the acceptance that there is sorrow in the world, from the time of birth to the time of death. The second is the truth of how dukkha, suffering is caused. According to the Buddha, the cause is tanha, craving which includes feelings like hatred, anger, lust, envy, and jealousy. The third is the truth of how dukkha, suffering ends by removing the force of incessant neediness in our lives. And the fourth describes the path leading to its removal by following the Noble Eightfold Path: right understanding, right thought, right speech, right action, right livelihood, right effort, right mindfulness and right concentration.

 Christianity

Christians share the view of the Hebrew Bible that originally God created a perfect world – a paradise where human beings were meant to live in harmony with one another and with responsibility for the whole of creation. But it is clear that something has gone radically wrong both in the world of nature and in human nature too. The story in the book of Genesis of Adam and Eve's disobedience expresses this sense that human beings have rebelled against God and have come into enmity with one another and even with their environment. There seems to be a flaw in the whole created order.

There are many examples throughout the Bible – in both the Hebrew Bible and the New Testament

– of bad things happening to good people. In the Book of Job in the Hebrew Bible and the Passion of Jesus in the Gospels, there is an investigation into why God allows such things to happen.

Christians would answer that God has given free will to human beings and that humanity, tempted by evil, personified as Satan, himself a 'fallen angel', has chosen to rebel against the laws of God, and has failed in its responsibility to care for the whole of creation. Therefore, natural disasters, human suffering and disease have been the inevitable outcome. But this does not mean that nothing can be done to relieve them. Jesus refused to blame human beings and say that sickness was the result of sin, but He himself healed the sufferers (John 9, 1–7). He commanded his followers to show compassion to the needy (Matthew 25, 31–40).

Christians believe that though God does not always intervene to prevent suffering, nevertheless in Christ He has intervened to share in human suffering. So nothing can be so bad that it separates us finally from the love of God revealed in the life, death and resurrection of Jesus Christ (Romans 8, 33–390).

> *I do question the fact that if there is a God, then why do bad things happen? Why is the world so unjust? Why is health and wealth distributed so unevenly across the different countries? I used to go to church every week since I was a baby. I didn't go for about one to two years whilst looking after my dad who has Alzheimer's as it was too difficult to take him. I did feel guilty about this. However I could have gone in the evening but didn't. But when I do attend church I feel peaceful. The hymns often make me quite emotional and I do shed tears thinking about my dad and other problems in life.*

> Vathani

 Hinduism

Many Hindus think that the bad things that happen to the individual are a consequence of karma – the law of reward and punishment that continues on from previous lives when we are re-born. Karma is a behaviour law and it works on the basis that human beings are self-conscious and can know if they are doing right things or not. According to Hindu tradition, our present condition, our happiness and status are directly the product of our previous life – our past karma. Consequently, we are responsible for our present condition and our future. Luck plays no part in life at all. We cannot say we have had good or bad luck in a lottery as whether we win or not has been determined in the past by our karma. We can have dukkha – bad experience in our lives and sukha – happy experience in our lives and it is up to us to decide how we will behave – our present karma – and it is on the basis of our past and present karma that God will decide what kind of re-birth we will have. It is only when we have a human re-birth as opposed to an animal, bird or plant re-birth that we can consider achieving moksha – escape from re-birth and union with God.

As far as natural disasters are concerned, the answer is the same. Life is planned on the day of conception according to the Will of God and nobody can change what happens to the individual. Some people will escape and some will suffer. Again, the only way to escape the suffering in the world is to achieve moksha and the only way to do that is through leading an honest life, being good to others, praying and meditating often guided by a good teacher.

> *It's difficult to know what to say about why bad things happen. I know if I sow mango seeds, I get mangos . . . so you get out what you put into life. But even if you are good here now and your present karma is fine, you don't know what your past karma was about . . . you may have*

done something awful and that's why something bad has happened now. I suppose I think whether it is something bad happening to me personally or a widespread national disaster like a flood or an earthquake, we somehow have to accept the Will of God.

Karmal

 Islam

The word 'Islam' means 'submission'. Many Muslims understand that the bad things that happen in life are a way of submitting to the will of Allah. Muslims do not know why bad things happen: it is only Allah, God who knows and human beings cannot know or understand the ways of Allah.

What Muslims do know is from the writings in the Qur'an that contains rules that can help to prevent doing bad things. The Qur'an affirms the existence of spiritual beings called jinn. Their purpose is to serve God. Rebellious jinn are called demons. The chief demon is Iblis, Satan whom Allah allows to tempt people to evil as a test of their faith. Many Muslims believe suffering strengthens faith, as pain often leads to repentance and prayer and good deeds. The Qur'an mentions many incidents of Allah using natural disasters as a way to maintain a balance of his natural laws or inflict a punishment on a population. The Prophet Muhammad appealed to Allah for protection against natural disasters. When the Prophet heard thunder and saw lightening, he said: 'My Lord, do not kill us with Your wrath and do not send us to perdition by inflicting suffering on us. Spare us all that, our Lord.'

An important teaching in the Qur'an is the doctrine of the Last Judgement. On the last day the whole of humanity will be raised to life and will appear before God to be judged and to be given a place in Paradise or Hell, depending on whether we have done mainly good or mainly bad things:

God is Supreme, he's the Creator. And we are his slaves. The Creator has created in this world a stage, an arena, in which men and women are tested by the works that they do. If they don't pass the test, they are punished but if they do pass it, then they return to God forever to be rewarded in paradise. We just accept suffering as part of the test. Good, bad, whatever happens during our life, our everyday life, we just take it as a part of our life.

Serena

 Judaism

According to the Jewish view of human nature, all people are born free of sin, with the ability to choose between good and evil. And the world in which people are placed is a good world, created by God for the benefit of humanity.

Jewish people have free choice as to the way they behave during life and thus are responsible for their own behaviour. Although God knows everything, how we respond is up to the individual, sometimes in partnership with God, as Eva explains:

One of the worst things that happened to me was when I got this injury on my foot and it stopped me from doing athletics which was my favourite thing . . . it was my escapism from everything else in life and I felt really frustrated and I just wanted to get back into it and I found it really difficult that I was being held back and I thought well that's the end I won't ever achieve anything again. But then I realised that I had to be positive about it . . . go out and get some treatment and start back slowly. In the end I did achieve what I wanted to achieve and got my personal best and did well and was able to carry on. I definitely think God helped me get through that . . . I go to synagogue regularly and I pray and I wanted to get better so that made me think that if I needed help then I had to be positive as well as ask God to help me get better.

Eva

As far as suffering is concerned, Jewish people believe that they cannot understand the ways of God and some believe that God suffers along side the sufferer, as when in the Nazi Holocaust six million Jews, gipsies and homosexuals were murdered. Jewish people believe that it is possible to eventually get rid of the suffering in the world by working to help those in need. This is the concept of *tikkun olam*, making the world a better place.

A sin is anything that is against God and therefore all the bad things that are carried out against other human beings are sins against God because according to Jewish teaching, human beings are created in the image of God. Being created in the 'image of God' means that every person in the world has the possibility of reflecting the goodness of God that is completely opposite to doing bad things. Following Jewish tradition there are three major categories of bad behaviour or sins: a het, doing something bad unintentionally; an avon, doing something bad intentionally; and a pesha, doing something bad for the sake of doing something bad. None of these three types of sin are unforgivable, but to be pardoned we must accept we have done wrong, make amends with the person we have wronged and then ask God's forgiveness and give charity (Isaacson, 1979: 152).

There is one day in the year Yom Kippur – The Day of Atonement when Jewish people fast and confess their collective sins, pray for forgiveness and vow to lead better lives in the year ahead. Before Yom Kippur there are ten days of repentance in which people speak directly to ask forgiveness of the person they have wronged in the past year.

 Sikhism

According to Sikhism, God created goodness. It is the absence of goodness which we have named evil or bad. And what we regard as bad has a special purpose that we do not understand. All we know is the bad things that happen test our characters and make us more aware of God. Guru Nanak, the founder of Sikhism, said in The Guru Granth Sahib (sacred scriptures) 'suffering is the remedy and comfort is a disease'. In other words, we may be able to use our difficulties to come closer to God whereas things that are easy for us may take us further away from God.

Natural disasters such as earthquakes are part of a cycle of births and re-births. These are all in God's great plan that we cannot easily understand. The more we meditate and study The Guru Granth Sahib the more we come to know of God's ways. According to Sikhism, first we have to become competent to understand then eventually we will be able to know the answers to those questions which we want to know. Life on this earth is undergoing continuous change – reproduction, evolution and destruction. How and when humanity joined this cycle and how long this will continue to be part of it, cannot be described definitely by anyone.

Bad things that happen to the individual are part of the same plan. We should do our duty assigned to us by God, i.e. to love God, his virtues and all his creatures. We should do our duty honestly, sincerely, and devotedly, neither being jealous of others nor full of our own ego. As well as Nam Japna (meditation), Kirath Karna (earning an honest living) and Vand Chakna (sharing our earnings with the needy), Sikhism provides teachings to prevent the individual from doing bad things. Teachings about the company we keep, lying, drinking, gambling, begging and back-biting.

In Sikhism it is possible to make amends when we have done something wrong. The person who has done wrong must be absolutely remorseful and ask for forgiveness and do good deeds to put things right. The Guru Granth Sahib keeps reminding us that if we take one step forward with body and soul towards God then God takes one hundred thousand steps forward to receive us. He is waiting for us, it is us who are keeping him at bay with lust, anger, greed, attachment and ego.

> *People, I believe, are good. That's my personal belief. Maybe that's an optimistic way of looking at things, but I want to follow a path of love and never want to judge a person. So, for this kind of question, 'Why do bad things happen to good people?' I just think that bad things happen to people. There's no doubt about it. It happens, whether they are good, or bad, in the eyes of God. So, the way I look at it is that I accept it. I question it and wonder why, but, in the end, I accept it, because this is what is meant to happen. For one, there is nothing we can do about it, like when someone passes away. I can cry about it all I want, but there is nothing I can do about it and it won't bring them back. So, we can express that sorrow, but, first and foremost, I would look at it and believe that everything happens for a reason. Maybe I won't understand that reason, but I do acknowledge and accept that this is all in the hands of God. He does choose what is best and I look at it in a positive light and I learn from it, if anything. If I can grow from it, I'll grow from it. If not, I accept it.*
>
> Paramjit

Strategies for moving on

This section of the chapter looks at strategies for moving on with our lives when bad things happen. It often takes time to recognise what can and cannot be solved. Once recognised we then have the opportunity to come to terms with the situation. Coming to terms means not indulging in either pointless guilt or resentment and bitterness. To accept that there is nothing to be done can lead to complete paralysis and giving up on self:

> *That's it . . . there's nothing I can do . . . there's nothing to say . . . I'll always be guilty . . . end of story.*
>
> Jodi

To accept the situation in a balanced way can lead to a fresh start:

> *I try really hard to think there's always light at the end of the tunnel . . . it's very easy to get bogged down with it but most of the time I think now . . . yes, I did this, I own it, I accept the consequences of the action and now I get on with dealing with the consequences and I forgive myself.*
>
> Rudi

In difficult situations, there is a depth of experience that potentially can be used to transform the problem into something useful. The experience may not always be positive but can sometimes become part of the search for meaning in our lives.

How this transformation takes place is in our hands. It may be that instead of blaming ourselves, other people and God; we can make use of our experience, of other people's experience or of our awareness of God to help when things go wrong.

Stop and Think: you/colleagues/young people

Here is a mind map with some positive techniques for moving on with life. Above the mind map, there are some questions to ask as a way of starting up a discussion with your colleagues and the young people with whom you work. Remember there is never one right answer and beware of evaluating other people's ideas too quickly. It is often more productive to consider the pros and cons before giving your own opinion. This may mean asking even more questions in a gently probing manner.

- Have you ever used any of these strategies?
- If so, when and why and how?
- If you haven't, pick one now and explain how you could use it for moving on with your life?
- Can you add more strategies for moving on with life?
- How could you pass on this kind of information to the young people you work with?

Positive thinking	God	Support from others
Role models		
	Getting involved with something new	
Using problems creatively		Realising the bigger picture
	Growing inside	
Forgiving ourselves		Forgiving others

Strategies for moving on

Below, there is a little detail on each strategy presented in the above mind map.

Positive thinking

What we say to ourselves dictates how we feel. The negative language that we use externally may well be what we say to ourselves internally. By challenging our internal dialogue, we can begin to change our feelings about our past experience. If we keep asking ourselves 'what do I want to achieve now' rather than re-living our memories of the bad events that happened in the past, there is more chance of a new start (Knight, 1997: 54).

Support from others

There are times when we need someone to talk to. Some people, like Consey, are naturally extrovert and always find some-one to talk things over with:

> *I'm a talker so I tend to talk to people and that helps to lift the burden . . . so by talking about it you get someone else's perspective on the situation and it does help.*

Consey

For others, it isn't so easy. Often there's no-one around who we know and even when there is, we are not always sure whether we should speak about what has happened. Sometimes, we may have to trust our instincts and try the person out by talking about something else. Then we can find out if the person is really listening in a non-judgemental way to what we are saying. If we are confident that this is the case and thus comfortable to speak about what is really on our mind, we may be able to use that person as a sounding board in order to clarify our thoughts.

Sometimes, we need more than a sounding board; it may be professional support for a specific problem. Where to find the appropriate person and/or organisation can be difficult. Beware of contacts through the internet – not all are qualified. Instead, the local surgery or Citizens Advice Bureau are often able to help to find the support that is necessary:

> *I had just stopped using heavy drugs – cocaine mainly, just once or twice – but I was using a lot of weed. My doctor thought it would be a good idea to go and see Group Nine, so she put me in touch with them. Through them I have recently been meeting a mentor through the Buddy Scheme. He has given me a lot of information about the drugs I have used. We went on a trip behind the scenes at the De La Warr Pavilion – it's just a chance to open your eyes to other things you could do in life except smoking drugs . . . I will knock it on the head . . . I want to make a nice home for myself.*

Jon

Role models

Thinking about how others cope encourages us to put our own problems into perspective. Many famous and non-famous people can give us inspiration to overcome difficulties. Like Ellen MacArthur who broke the world record for the number of days it took her to sail alone around the world. Many times she was in extreme danger: her back-up generator caused fumes in the cabin; she battled against icebergs, mountainous waves, sub-zero temperatures and fierce storms. When she arrived home triumphant but absolutely exhausted she spoke about the highs and lows of being at sea. She explained that just like in life generally, living on her yacht was a balance between painfully difficult situations and extremely joyful ones. 'I've put everything in – my heart, my soul, my flesh, my blood, just everything. I've never pushed this hard', she wrote in her online journal on January 25th 2005.

Gil is not famous but he has inspired his sister Sue to deal with her pain:

> *My brother is a down-syndrome child . . . he has given me insight into real love and kindness. He has helped to make me who I am . . . the sort of person that can cope with the pain I am going through at the moment . . . I know if he can live as he does and give so much joy to everyone . . . then I've got no excuse.*

Sue

Getting involved with something new

Coming to terms with something bad may involve distancing ourselves from the past and looking at new ways to make life worthwhile. Something new may be something we've always wanted to do but have never got round to or it could be developing skills such as computer skills in order to find more opportunities in the work-place. Doing something different may give us a chance to meet new people and make new friends who do not know about our past difficulties.

> *I've started playing netball. It really takes me out of myself. I come home feeling differently about things. I think it's the running around that clears my head and I enjoy being part of this great group of people. It's beginning to make a difference.*

Ahlam

Using problems creatively

Creativity can become an outlet for our pent-up emotions. Some people incorporate their past problems within a creative form: art work, writing, acting, music, etc. For example, if you like to write you could use some of the difficulties you have encountered in a short story. The story does not have to be identical; the names of the people and places are often changed.

Sometimes, by playing out the problem in a different way, we reach an acceptance of what has happened and begin to understand that it is not necessarily something external over which we have no control. It may also help us to find some meaning and value in the difficulty.

Realising the bigger picture

We as individuals are one part of an enormous world with many problems. Looking around us we see great joy and great sadness. Perhaps, we are not necessarily entitled to be in a happy state all the time. In fact, if nothing bad ever happened to us how would we appreciate the good times? It is often the contrast that enables us to realise what is positive in our lives.

> *I don't think I'll ever get over Berry's death. But also generally I grieve for the world. I don't see how you can possibly be 100 per cent happy. I never have been and I know I never will. I think modern society is geared to thinking you are entitled to be happy, and it's such a shock when horrid things happen, but if you take it that life is really a test . . . you know, a test to see if you can get through it . . . then it's all right, and then when you do have joyful moments, like last night, with these kids, you think, yeah, how lucky I am.*
>
> Lilla

God

The concept of God has been around since time immemorial. People who believe in God have always said that God gives comfort and direction when bad things happen:

> *I became very ill and eventually discovered it was cancer. When the doctors looked at my family medical history, they realised there was a genetic link between the causes of death of my uncle and my brother and my own illness. My family thought it was just random bad luck. I feel God is walking alongside me helping me to cope and I get a lot of comfort from that. I've got big decisions to make about whether I'm going to have a family or not but I have the feeling that with God with me I think I'll be able to take the right decisions.*
>
> Ruby

Forgiving others

When things have gone wrong with a particular person who is still alive, it may help to think about forgiving that person. In trying to forgive, we don't necessarily forget what happened but we may well let go of at least some part of the original anger and hurt and desire to punish the person who hurt us. This is never easy. But it is certainly possible and may be helped by a number of factors. It is far easier to forgive if in the past we valued the relationship we had with the other person. Then we may be able to weigh this particular upset on the scales of the relationship as a whole.

In order to forgive we need to understand what happened from the point of view of the other person. We need to try to find a way of saying: 'What you did really hurt me. Why did you do it?' It may emerge that we ourselves are largely to blame; perhaps we were blind to the pain caused by the way we behaved. Or we may realise, on reflection, that the other person was under a lot of pressure, and this may help us to re-evaluate their behaviour. Understanding does not take the past away, but it can transform it retroactively. The events are now seen as part of a rather different story and we no longer feel the same hurt. This change may take hours, months or years but through it we come to see the past in a new light, and in so doing set the scene for the future; for a potentially positive new relationship.

Forgiving ourselves

There are, of course, situations where it is not possible to forgive the person who has hurt us. The person may no longer be alive or may be extremely stubborn and unyielding, in which case we may decide to end the connection. But we are still left with the process of trying to come to terms with what happened. We can choose our response to any given situation, and the first step is to recognise our feelings. Practice observing the emotional state rather than being it.

Understanding and letting go of hurt and indignation are always a struggle. But if we do not try, we often end up twisting the knife into our own wounds and becoming the victim, not only of what others did to us, but of our own attitude as well:

I've been angry with her for so long and it's made me a real miserable person I can't remember how long . . . I've made my life and my family's a real nightmare . . . I know it's time to move on now. I've punished myself for long enough.

Amir

Growing inside

Growing inside and gaining insight is potentially one of the positive side effects of hard times. Eventually, after the internal battle to overcome the repercussions of the problem, we may be able to use the experience to help others.

Many times we learn something more about ourselves and other people because of what we have been through. For example, Daniel believes that although it has taken a long time, the terrible thing that happened to him – his father's tragic death – has in some way helped him to grow inside and to relate to other people in a more meaningful way:

I suppose in a funny kind of a way, I've used the difficulty. My father was shot in Zambia when I was six years old. He was brought back to England and lay unconscious in hospital for months . . . eventually he died . . . I had to really battle with myself to make myself talk to people when I was growing up. I had to get over loads of jealous feelings I had when I saw other kids with their dads . . . I had to use the negative situations and try to do something with them . . . now looking back at my childhood, all those experiences have helped me to relate to other people and to get the most out of other people and out of myself.

Daniel

Chapter 5

Is There a God?

This chapter and the remaining chapters of this book provide an opportunity to learn about beliefs that we do not necessarily share. In our multi-cultural and multi-faith society it is essential to try to understand people with different ideas and traditions from ourselves. If we steer clear of people who talk or dress differently and if we only mix with people who think the same as we do, it is relatively easy to be frightened and superstitious of others.

You may be absolutely certain that God exists or you may be just as sure that God does not exist. Or you may not know one way or the other. There are many degrees between belief and non-belief. But, you don't have to believe in God to think about the idea of God: an idea that has occupied the human mind throughout time. People have always questioned the existence and nature of God and nowadays neuro-scientists are even trying to discover if part of the brain focuses specifically on godly matters.

This chapter looks at a few of the very many different opinions and beliefs about God: pre-historic and Ancient Greek views as well as what six of the world's religions have to say. With the help of 'Stop and Think' points, this chapter hopes to stimulate an ongoing conversation between you and your colleagues and between you and the young people with whom you work.

Stop and Think: you

Before you read this chapter, here is a questionnaire for you to do by yourself in order to question your own ideas about God. Take your time – you may not be able to answer all the questions but try. Think about how your response is coloured by your life experience, personality and upbringing.

Questionnaire

Do you think there is a God?   **Yes/no/not sure**

If the answer is no or not sure, answer the following questions:

- Do you remember when and where you first heard about the idea of God?
- If so, do you remember what you thought at that time, e.g. did you instantly think it was a load of rubbish or were you curious?
- What do you mean by God?
- Do you believe in something other than God?
- If so, what is it?
- Does that belief affect your life?
- How?
- Is God another word for nature?
- Is God another word for conscience?

- What do tragedies such as the Asian Tsunami, which killed over 300,000 people, make you think about God?
- Have any moments in your life made you think there might be something or someone guiding you?
- If so, what were those moments?
- How do you feel now about those moments?

If the answer is yes, then answer the following questions:

- Do you remember when and where you first heard about the idea of God?
- If so, do you remember what you thought at that time, e.g. did you instantly believe or did you think it was a load of rubbish?
- What do you mean by God?
- Why do you believe in God?
- What is your God like? e.g. is your God a personal God unconnected with a faith tradition or is your God connected with a faith tradition?
- What are the consequences to you personally of a belief in God?
- Is God a super power that made and controls the world?
- If yes, how does God do it?
- If no, how do you think the world began?
- Think about the times you have felt 'close to God'. Is there a common element, a sense of progress or an old idea revisited?
- If so, what is it?
- Do you talk to God about every day matters?
- Does God speak to you?
- If yes, how?
- If your God is full of goodness, how do you account for earthquakes, famine and floods that kill countless people?

Pre-historic gods

There is archaeological evidence that pre-historic human beings believed in divine supernatural forces. There are many theories why. One theory is the need of the pre-historic 'male' (as opposed to the pre-historic 'female') to believe in the divine. For the pre-historic 'male' it made sense to believe that some divine supernatural force linked with the female who gave birth was the answer to the question: *where do I come from?* So in the search for *where do I come from?* the female was elevated to the position of the divine because of her ability to create life in the biological and physical sense. When the male began to understand the part he played in procreation, the idea of the female's divinity diminished. At the same time, the male sex begins to dominate with the realisation that women and children depend on men to hunt for food to sustain the family.

But the psychological need for God does not seem to go away. The search focuses on creating gods that carry traits of nature. We can see in many ancient cultures and primal religions – the religions of small scale pre-literate societies – that gods are made in the image of nature. Gods like these often live in rivers and lakes, in the sky and stars, on and under the earth. People who follow the primal religions often live near to nature and are at the mercy of natural disasters: storms, floods, famine, disease, fire and earthquakes. They are also at the mercy of other hostile groups. And death is a very common event and can come tragically early. Worshipping gods is a way of saying that nature and feelings are connected with an invisible reality that is greater than the human being.

Many primal religions also have a 'great god' who has won a heroic victory over the other gods. It may be a god who lives in heaven far away from people and is hardly worshipped. It is believed that this god created the world and is the source of moral law. He is all-seeing and all-knowing and he can be both kind and cruel.

In Ankole, Uganda, the Nkore people believe in Ruhanga the Creator who made all things at once. Ruhanga is personal yet distant. He is the principle of order and is therefore good, but he is reluctant to intervene directly in the affairs of humans. This belief recurs in African religions as the following myth from West Africa shows:

> There was once a woman who had a very long pestle, and when she pounded her corn the wooden pole hit against God who lived just above the sky. One day she gave a great bang, hitting God in the eye, and in anger he went away into the distance, never to return.

Langley, 1993: 16

Ancient Greek gods

In the more urban setting of the Ancient Greek cities, the gods and demi-gods are given human traits: Zeus represents power, strength and lust, Hera, Zeus's wife is the home maker, Athena wisdom, Apollo creativity and Aphrodite love and beauty, and so on. Both positive and negative aspects of human nature are demonstrated in the gods but the reality of living life with these gods is an unforgiving, negative one. There is no redemption (forgiveness for past wrongs), only retribution (punishment inflicted for past wrongs). If a human does something wrong, revenge is taken for what is considered to be hubris – insult to the gods. There is no possibility of atonement followed by forgiveness. For example, as told in Sophocles' play, Oedipus kills his father by accident but he is punished without the possibility of forgiveness. He had committed hubris and revenge had to be taken (March, 2000: 283).

In these examples of pre-historic and ancient Greek gods, we see that people develop an understanding of God that fits in with their specific spiritual needs. And spiritual needs change according to time and place. When the male was dependent on the female, the female was divine. When men and women were dependent on the land, the gods show characteristics of nature. When human beings were anthropocentric – centred on themselves – the gods show characteristics of human beings. Later with the birth of Judaism and the creation of monotheism – the belief in one God – there is a greater interest in the opportunity of redemption – forgiveness for past wrongs.

Stop and Think: you/colleagues

- Have your ideas about God changed according to your circumstances?
- How is God used as an explanation for the bits of life we don't understand?
- If humanity did not exist, what would be the point of God's existence?

Ideas about God today

I have always believed in God but have questioned this within the last five years. I don't rely on religion and don't necessarily believe that praying will get me anywhere even though I was told when I was young that if you do not ask you won't get. However, in times of feeling scared and wanting help I do 'talk' to God and ask for help.

Vathani

Religion, whether you follow a particular one or not, is a good place to start when you want to find out about God. There are two major faith traditions in the world today. Both of them – the Eastern Salvationist or Mystical Tradition and the Western Prophetic Tradition deny the materialist view of the world – the idea that this world is all there is. Instead the essentially spiritual nature of reality is emphasised. Although there is undoubtedly an overlap, a rough division can be made between ideas about God within the Western Prophetic tradition and ideas about God within the Eastern Salvationist or Mystical tradition.

The Western Prophetic Tradition

The Prophetic tradition springs from a parent Semitic group – peoples descended from Shem (see Genesis, 10: 21) whose religions include Judaism, Christianity, Islam and their offshoots. The Prophetic tradition stresses the prophetic – God reveals His will to us through an agent: a prophet such as Moses in the Hebrew Bible and Muhammad in the Qur'an. The books in which these prophets appear are sacred and have authority over the lives of their readers. For Christians the words of Jesus have authority because he is considered to be an expression of God.

 Judaism

Judaism is monotheistic: Jewish people believe there is only one God with no intermediary. He is the God of everyone, whether they are Jewish or not. He is infinitely powerful and knowledgeable; the sole Creator and Sustainer of the universe. God is formless: anthropomorphisms – human forms – found in the Hebrew Bible are merely symbolic, a literary device used to emphasise some aspect of God's character. For example, in Deuteronomy 14, 34 the strength of God's resolve to take the Children of Israel out of Egypt is symbolised by 'a mighty hand and by an outstretched arm'.

God is transcendent – independent of the material world and at the same time immanent – permanently pervading the material world. God is holy and perfect in all his ways.

Hear, O Israel, the Lord our God, the Lord is One. And you shall love the Lord, your God with all your heart, and with all your soul, and with all your might.

From the Hebrew Bible (Old Testament) Deuteronomy 6: 4–5

Abraham was the first known person to accept the idea of one God (see Book of Genesis, Chapters 12 and 13). Later Moses (1300 Before Common Era (BCE)) is given the Ten Commandments by God. The first two statements of the Ten Commandments declare:

I am the Lord your God, who brought you out of the land of Egypt, out of the house of bondage. You shall have no other gods before me. You shall not make for yourself a carved image, or any likeness of anything that is in heaven above, or that is in the earth beneath, or that is in the water under the earth; you shall not bow down to them nor serve them.

From the Hebrew Bible (Old Testament) Exodus 20: 2–4

From this commandment and many other warnings in the Hebrew Bible, Jewish people are not allowed to worship any representation of God. The name of God is considered so holy that it is never spoken or written down. The Hebrew letters yud, hay, yud, hay represent God's name. This is known as the tetragrammaton – the four letter sacred word for God. When the tetragrammaton appears in the Hebrew Bible or in the liturgy, 'Adonai' (the Hebrew word for 'Lord') is said instead.

I do think that there is a God that exists . . . I definitely think there is someone . . . sometimes on a Friday night, when the candles flicker I just think that God's there helping and watching over me. I think He guides me a lot . . . if I wasn't Jewish and I didn't believe in anything then I wouldn't have a path to follow, a route to go . . .I just feel that I'm never alone that God is with me, helping me along, helping me to make my decisions.

Eva

 *Christianity*

Christians believe in one God, but this unity contains three Persons: the Father (God, Creator), the Son (Jesus, Saviour) and the Holy Spirit (the Energy) that empowers people to work together in community with one another. The three persons are distinct from one another, yet not divided. They work in perfect unison and they are never in conflict with each other. The Son, Jesus Christ is revealed in John's Gospel in the New Testament as the Word who was 'with God' in the beginning and yet 'was God.' (John 1: 1)

God means to me the person that I answer to . . . the one who's in charge like a father. He's like the number one – the top man – He's the person that if I have a problem or a worry I'll turn to Him. I try to do the right things and stay on the straight and narrow for Him. I respect Him. The Holy Spirit is inside me – it's like right in the centre – my conscience. Jesus is the one in between me and God.

Consey

The God of Christianity is the God of Abraham, Isaac and Jacob of the Old Testament (Hebrew Bible). He is so holy and flawless that he cannot be tempted with evil, neither does he tempt any man (see the Letter of James 1: 13-14). There is no negative, evil or dark side to his nature (see the First Letter of John 1: 5). God is transcendent: existing above and beyond this material world. Yet he is also immanent: actively involving himself in this world and making himself accessible to everyone through belief in him (see the Letter of Paul to the Ephesians 3: 14–9).

Through the example and teachings of Jesus, God is especially revealed as the 'heavenly Father' who is motivated by a deep concern for humanity. The apostle John explained, 'God so loved the world that he gave his only begotten Son, so that everyone who believes in Him may not perish but have everlasting life' (John 3: 16).

Idolatry is prohibited in Christianity. Some branches of Christianity such as Catholicism use statues and icons, though not in the same sense as idols. Other Christian sects speak against this practice as being non-biblical and idolatrous.

Islam

Islam is monotheistic, teaching that Allah is the one Supreme Being: the only true God. God has no partner or equal. The word 'Allah' in Arabic cannot be plural and is neither male nor female.

> *Say! He is God. The One and Only!*
> *God, the Eternal: He begot none, nor was He begotten.*
> *None is equal to Him.*

Qur'an: 112

Allah has many names, all of which describe divine attributes – the characteristics of God – such as the Living, the Eternal, the Supreme, the Tremendous, the Merciful and the Compassionate. Allah is transcendent – existing apart from and beyond the range of the material universe and perfect in all His ways.

Though Allah is a personal God, His ways are incomprehensible to human beings. Allah does not speak directly to human beings. He sends His word through messengers known as prophets. Allah's most important and final messenger was Muhammad ibn Abdullah (Muhammad son of Abdullah) born in Mecca in Saudi Arabia 570 Common Era (CE). Whilst near Mecca in meditation, Muhammad received the first of the divine revelations from Allah. Around 610 CE Muhammad began preaching that he was the messenger of the One True God Allah – the same God worshipped in the Jewish and Christian religions.

> *There is a hadith – a saying that how ever much you love your children, God will love you 72 times more than that and if you can pinpoint that love then you are half way there. I think for me the notion of God is that I'm being looked after. That I feel secure in the knowledge that God is there in every single thing and that's why they say Islam is a way of life. God will tell me the etiquette of sleeping, the etiquette of eating, the etiquette of greeting somebody . . . He completely rules my life and without that I'm lost . . . it's a constant God consciousness in everything that you do is very, very important . . . it holds you . . . you're grounded and not searching . . . you know exactly what to do . . . to know that through good and bad God is always there to help you through sorrow through happiness and the first person you see or you think of or you want to pray to is God and it's something that controls your every move but in a good way not in a way that you feel restricted.*

Anisa

The Eastern tradition

The Eastern tradition springs from a parent Indian root that includes Hinduism, Buddhism, Sikhism and their offshoots. The Eastern tradition stresses finding God inside the human spirit. Life on earth involves a mystical journey – a system of spirituality aimed at achieving direct intuitive experience of God. It is a spiritual journey that has many stages on the way and may involve fasting, meditation and prayer. It is hoped that eventually the soul of the human being returns to God. Many of the Eastern traditions seek to free the soul from the endless cycle of re-birth or reincarnation to which it is subjected in this world.

Hinduism

The Hindu religion says that all gods – Hindu or others – are facets of the One God. God is known as Brahman. Brahman is represented by the holy trinity formed by Brahma, Vishnu and Shiva. Brahma is the creator who brings the Universe into existence: Vishnu preserves life and all living things; Shiva is the destroyer who destroys the world. This ongoing cycle of creation, preservation and destruction is at the centre of Hindu belief.

Many Hindus follow either Vishnu or Shiva who both have various forms, male and female with different powers and interests. Worshippers choose which form to pray to depending on what they want to achieve. Vishnu has come to earth in ten forms including two human forms – Rama and Krishna. Rama and Krishna represent different aspects of God. Rama is the ideal ruler and illustrates the responsibilities of the leader in society and Krishna is renowned as a warrior, teacher and lover:

> *I am happy that my God has many names and faces. Different people refer to my father by different names depending on their relationship with him and at different times of the day or week he dresses to suit the occasion depending on his needs. But my father is the same person. In the same way, different Hindus believe in one supreme being, who also is known by many different names and appears in many different forms to meet the task required.*
>
> Deepak

According to Hinduism, God is neither male nor female. God is as much 'She' – the mother of the universe as God is 'He' – the father of the universe. God is the Great Force and the holy trinity of Brahma, Vishnu and Shiva is represented by the sacred word 'Aum'. 'Aum' is abbreviated to 'Om' and is repeated in prayer to bring the worshipper closer to God.

AUM
　A = Body = Brahma the Creator
　U = Soul = Vishnu the Preserver
　M = Spirit = Shiva the Destructor

> *I am the same to all beings, and my love is ever the same; but those who worship me with devotion, they are in me and I in them.*
>
> Bhagavad Gita 9: 29

 Buddhism

Buddhism does not believe in the idea of one creator God. The founder of Buddhism, Siddhartha Gautama, who lived in India about 2,500 years ago, acknowledged the existence of minor gods in the universe but he insisted that they, like all other living beings, are caught within the round of continual birth and death. These minor gods like all other living beings have to experience and find the answer to the sufferings of sickness, old age and death within themselves. Siddhartha Gautama placed birth as a human being above all other existences, since it is in this form that one could make progress in understanding the true nature of life.

Siddhartha Gautama gained enlightenment and understanding of the truth about the way things are and thus becoming the Buddha, 'the enlightened one'. According to Buddhism, a Buddha is a person who discloses the truth to others and so enables them to understand their true nature. Buddhists do not worship the Buddha as a god but as an exceptional human being. Buddhists believe that he was one of many Buddhas, past and present and future. Buddhists consider that by meditation, self-discipline and effort a person may gain insight, wisdom and eventually become enlightened like the Buddha himself.

> *As a mother cares for her son,*
> *Her only son, all her days.*
> *So towards all things living*
> *A man's mind should be all-embracing.*
>
> (Karaniya) Metta Sutta, Suttanipata,149 (Translation: Discourse on Loving-kindness)

There are many different Buddhist groups and they vary in their understanding of the existence of gods. For example, Zen and Theravadan schools of Buddhism believe that there is no god who can help a person to achieve enlightenment. Pure Land Buddhists worship Amida (Amitabha) Buddha who was originally a monk as a personal saviour. Nichiren Buddhists believe that Nichiren, a 13th-century Japanese monk, is a reincarnation of Jogyo Bosatsu. According to this sect, Jogyo was a bodhisattva – one who attains Buddhahood but is not yet fully enlightened and thus not yet free from reincarnation – cycle of re-births.

Vajrayana including Tibetan Buddhism promotes worshipful devotion to a long line of Dalai Lamas. The most recent one, Tenzin Gyatso, is the fourteenth and is presently exiled from Tibet. All Dalai Lamas are considered to be bodhisattvas, as well as incarnations of their predecessors. Tibetan Buddhists worship a pantheon of innumerable Buddhas, bodhisattvas, gods, goddesses and divine beings.

Here is Tenzin Chozom's personal opinion about God:

> *As far as Buddhism is concerned, it depends what you mean by God as to if I believe in Him. If God means infinite compassion, infinite omnipresence, always knowing, absolutely understand-ing of all beings . . . then that is what is described in Buddhist texts . . . Buddha knows perfectly how to help all beings and He's always active. I would say that now I feel that God and Buddha is the same thing . . . but it took me a few years to say this. I went through a bad phase thinking, oh my goodness there's no Buddha, there is no God.*
>
> Tenzin Chozom

 Sikhism

Sikhs believe in God, as revealed to the founder, Guru (spiritual leader or teacher) Nanak, born in 1469 CE. Guru Nanak and his successors taught that God is the eternal teacher and although known by many names, God is one. Among God's many characteristics are Wahiguru – wonderful teacher, Satguru – true teacher, Karta Purakh – creator and Akal Purakh – everlasting teacher. The name Wahiguru is often used when thinking and talking about God and this name is also used in meditation.

Guru Nanak describes God in the Mool Mantra – the basic creed – at the very beginning of the Sikh Holy Scripture, the Guru Granth Sahib:

> *God is only One*
> *His name is True*
> *He is the Creator*

He is Fearless
He is without an enemy
He never dies
He is beyond birth and death
He is self-existent
He is achieved by the grace of the true Guru

In one of the five daily Sikh prayers, the night prayer Kirtan Sohila says 'There is but One though your forms be unnumbered, Guru of gurus, Creator of all'. Another verse stresses, 'From nothingness the Formless One assumes a form, the Attribute-free becomes full of attributes.' (Guru Granth Sahib, 940). In other words, God created everything – the planets, the stars, plants, insect, animals and human beings and everything God created carries his reflection.

Sikhs do not believe in image worship or in gods and goddesses. Sikhs believe the only way to God is through Nam Jupna – meditation, Kirath Kurna – earning an honest living and Wond Chakna – sharing your earnings with the needy.

I believe there is one God and feel I can reach God through the Gurus' hymns and through repeating God's name. I can feel something inside me, there's some power, when I repeat His name . . . I just want to carry on . . . I just want to repeat it and repeat it.

Harjinder

Stop and Think: you/colleagues

- How tenable is the view held by some religious people that all other views apart from their own are wrong? Talk about, if possible, with people of different faiths.
- How can all views about God be right?
- As scientists find out more and more about the beginnings of life on earth, are we any nearer identifying the 'cause' or the 'prime mover'?
- Can a belief in God help us to improve ourselves and to improve the world we live in? How?
- Why is God often referred to as male?

Activity: colleagues/young people

Thoughts About God

Purpose: To think about and share ideas about the concept of God.
Preparation: Photocopy 'Thoughts About God' Handout.
Method: Break group into pairs or small groups.
                  Choose appropriate statements for your group participants according to their age and interest.
                  Invite group members to discuss the questions that follow.
                  A spokesperson from each group reports back to whole group.

'Thoughts About God' Handout

God is alive and well otherwise we wouldn't be here.

(Gill)

Questions to talk about:
Do you think this is true?
If so, why?
If not, why?

God is an old man with a white beard.

(Jay)

Questions to talk about:
Is this the image you have of God?
If so, why do you think you have this image?
If not, how do you imagine God?

In God's name, terrible things are done like the killing of children because they do not belong to a particular race or religion.

(Salma)

Questions to talk about:
How is it possible to believe in God when terrible things happen?
Where is God when these things happen?

In God's name, remarkable things are achieved like Mahatma Gandhi's peaceful struggle to bring equality to the women of India.

(Rudi)

Questions to talk about:
Do you think Mahatma Gandhi would have achieved the same if he did not believe in God?
How could God have helped him?
Are people generally more likely to believe in God when good things happen?

I won't be happy until I'm as famous as God

(Pop celebrity, Madonna, 2000)

Questions to talk about:
Is God famous?
If so, why ?
What does this statement say about Madonna?
Would fame make you happy?

I experienced a time of acute personal suffering in my late teens and it was then I realised that the Christian God is a God who himself entered into the suffering of the world, so as to redeem it – to take away the sins of the world.

(Langley, 1993: 94)

Question to talk about:
What are the sins of the world?
How can God take them away?
How can God feel personal pain?
Has God ever helped you when you were in trouble?
If so, how?
Is the Christian God similar to your God?

I believe in God as highest value, and I believe in a connection between all living things – humans, animals and the land. God as highest value does not imply a literal being – we cannot know if God exists – but we can know what it is to want more than materialism and pragmatism. We can use the idea of God to hoist ourselves out of smallness.

(Author Jeanette Winterson, *The Guardian*, 2001)

Questions to talk about:
Do you think God is 'highest value'?
If so, why?
If not, what is your 'highest value'?
Do you have values in your life that are not associated with your own well being?
If so, what values are they?
What do you want other than material things?
What do you value most in your life?

God's existence cannot be proved by argument, it must be accepted in faith

(Danish theologian and philosopher, Soren Kierkegaard 1813–55)

Questions to talk about:
Do you think we can know if God exists?
If God's existence can be proved by argument, what sort of argument would it be?
What argument can you give for the non-existence of God?
Is faith the same as belief in the existence of God?
If not, what is faith?

Humans project a notion of God to make their own wishes and interests appear legitimate and capable of fulfilment.

(German philosopher and poet, Friedrick Nietzsche 1844–1900)

Questions to talk about:
What does this mean?
What does this say about God?

Do you think it is true?

If so, why?

If not, why?

If there is no God, everything is permitted.

(Russian revolutionary and writer, Dostoevsky 1821–1881)

Questions to talk about:

Do you think that without God there are no rules for living?

Where do you get your ideas about how to live your life?

Does God tell you what is right and what is wrong?

How?

If you love God, you love science as well.

(Leila)

Questions to talk about:

Why is this the case?

What has science to do with God?

What has God to do with science?

Do you see a connection between science and the experience of God?

Do you see a connection between art and the experience of God?

Why do you think artists and musicians have religious experiences?

Are they perhaps in touch with the unseen world?

Chapter 6

What Happens Next?

Death education begins soon after life begins: television presents death in living colour every day. A pet is killed, a funeral procession passes, a bomb explodes, a close friend dies. Events like these can cause us to question the meaning of our lives and to ask ourselves what happens when life ends – what happens next?

This chapter takes a glimpse at what science, philosophy and religion have to say about the question: 'is there life after death?' Throughout the chapter young people talk about their experiences and there are 'Stop and Think' points for you and the young people with whom you work.

In many cultures, elaborate provision is made for the journey of the soul to the next world. Kings' corpses are surrounded by their finest possessions and even paupers may be buried with 'a penny for the ferryman' who will see them safely across the river to the other side. Stories, songs and paintings abound trying to give form to the formless and shape to our imaginings.

As far as we know, human beings are the only species who wonder whether or not they survive death. Why do we do this? Why do human beings ask the unanswerable question: is there life after death? On one hand, you may think it's because we just can't face the reality of our own non-existence. You may agree with the poet Philip Larkin who in his last major poem wrote that religion is a 'vast, moth-eaten, musical brocade Created to pretend we never die' (*Aubade,* first published Times Literary Supplement, 1985) and that notions of an after life are part of this pretence, this weak-minded self-deception. On the other hand, you may feel that each human consciousness is not merely a function of the chemical brain but suggests a larger, enduring consciousness. Another poet, William Wordsworth, coined the phrase 'intimations of immortality' to describe those echoes from another world which we hear faintly from time to time reminding us of some sort of otherness, some sort of elsewhere, just out of reach but waiting to be reclaimed (Quiller-Couch, 1946: 626).

Or you may just love ghost stories! You may feel there are too many accounts of people seeing ghosts or having out-of-the-body experiences to dismiss them as nonsense. Today, television channels and numerous web-sites deal solely with the paranormal. Even if they're money-spinning hoaxes, they are evidence of our fascination with the topic. The writer C.S. Lewis posed a logical question: how come our environment meets all our needs except the desire for immortality? We get hungry – there's food; we need to sleep – there's time to rest; we need love – we have families and friends. We are perfectly matched to our environment except in this one respect. Unless, of course, there **is** life after death.

Stop and Think:

- Do you think that when you die you no longer exist in any way whatsoever?
- Have you or do you know someone who has seen a ghost or had an out-of-the-body experience?
- What happened?
- What meaning do you give to this experience?

Neuro-scientists, psychologists, philosophers and theologians all have something to say about death. The neuro-scientist asks the question how do we die – what happens to the electrical impulses in the dying and the dead brain? How does that relate to the nature of the living brain and our day-to-day thoughts and feelings? Scientific research tells us how it feels to die. In a Dutch study recorded in *The Guardian* newspaper more than 60 out of 344 patients declared clinically dead and then resuscitated, could recall aspects of their near-terminal experience. Several reported elements of the classic near death experience, including tunnels of light, floating outside the body and seeing their life flash before their eyes. Variously interpreted as glimpses of the afterlife, or the soul's journey from the body, these experiences suggest to psychologists that the 'tunnel of light' results from a final surge of activity in the oxygen-starved brain's visual cortex – the outer grey matter of the brain.

Through science, as resuscitation techniques improve, more of us are likely to remember how it feels to die. But knowing how we die does not help us to answer the many questions that surround death. For example, do we completely disappear from this world or do we have a spirit that lives on?

> *I think that although my father died years ago, he still influences me in the things I like doing and what I want to do. I like the Hebrew singing in the synagogue because I remember how much he enjoyed it. I want to be good at my work because I want him to be proud of me. When I say my prayers I always thank God for him as if he was still here. I feel as if his spirit is within me.*
>
> Danielle

The idea that the human spirit lives on in the minds and memories of the living implies a connection to the past and to the future of the whole of humanity. If this is the case, we then have a collective existence that goes beyond our own specific life span. And we will continue to influence and be influenced by others. Like an individual tree that may die but the nutrients from that tree go back into the earth from which the next tree will grow.

Stop and Think:

- Do you think there is such a thing as the human spirit?
- If so, what do you think it is?
- Do you think that people's spirits live on after their death?
- If so, how?
- Are you influenced by anyone who has died?
- Do you think that you will influence other people after you die?
- How?

Carl Jung's Theory of Inherent Patterns of Expression

Some of the theories of the psychologist Carl Jung (1875–1961) fit comfortably with the view that the human spirit passes on into another person after death. According to Jung, the collective unconscious predates the individual and contains all our religious and spiritual experiences. The collective unconscious is the inherited modes of expression, feeling, thought and memory that all human beings are born with. Jung distinguishes between the personal unconscious and the collective unconscious mind. The personal unconscious is the set of repressed feelings and thoughts experienced and developed during an individual's lifetime. The collective unconscious by contrast is universal. It cannot be built up like an individual's personal unconscious but relies upon the people who lived before us (Carvalho, 1990: 74).

Jung calls these inherited and typical modes psychological archetypes. Archetypes are the patterns that form the basic blueprint for the most important parts of the human personality. For Jung, archetypes pre-exist in the collective unconscious. They repeat themselves eternally in the psyches of human beings and they determine how we both perceive and behave. These patterns are inborn within us. They reside as energy within the collective unconscious and are part of the psychological life of all peoples everywhere at all times. So it is possible to view the collective unconscious as the human spirit that is forever present even when we die.

Carl Jung's ideas are not new. The collective unconscious that contains universal feelings, thoughts and memory reflects something of Plato's idea of eternal, ideal forms.

Plato's Theory of Eternal Ideal Forms

The ancient Greek philosopher Plato (428–354 BCE) living some two thousand five hundred years before Carl Jung, suggested that there are eternal ideal forms – archetypes outside space or time that are part of our inheritance as human beings. According to Plato, there are two worlds: the world of absolute, perfect unchanging ideal forms and the world of ordinary, everyday experiences. Every form whether it is an abstract idea like 'truth' or a material fact like 'horse' is the ideal form that we have always known in our unconscious. For example, Plato said the word 'horse' refers not to a particular horse but to any horse. There is, somewhere or other, an ideal 'horse' outside space or time that is real, true and permanent. The particular 'horse' is not real in the same way as it is born, lives and dies and is part of our changeable, unstable day-to-day existence (Angeles, 1992: 114).

Stop and Think:

- What do Plato's 'eternal ideal forms' and Jung's 'inherent patterns of expression' have to do with the idea that the spirit of the human being lives on after death?
- How do these ideas overlap?

The idea that the spirit of the human being lives on after death is an important part of the philosophical and theological concept of reincarnation – the belief that individual souls survive death and are re-born to live again in a different body. In this way, life flows on and on through many existences. In many of the religions within the Eastern Salvationist or Mystical Tradition (Hinduism, Sikhism, etc.) the ultimate aim is complete separation of the soul from the body. At which time, the soul becomes one with God.

Stop and Think:

- Is freeing our souls from our bodies a way of freeing us from our 'selfishness'?
- What is our 'selfishness'?
- Is our 'selfishness' our concerns for our own material well-being?
- Is there anything wrong with that?
- If so, why?
- If not, why?

The other major faith tradition known as the Western Prophetic Tradition (Judaism, Christianity, Islam) argue that we have one earthly lifetime in order to find and become one with God. Western religions say that body and soul are together, and death is only their temporary separation. The soul lives on at death and on the Day of Judgement it will be reunited with its body, perhaps in some new spiritual form.

Stop and Think:

- How can the soul live on until reunited with the body?
- Where does the soul stay until reunited with the body?
- What do you think happens on the Day of Judgement?
- Do you think our bodies resurrect themselves?

The Western Salvationist Tradition

Traditionally, Jews, Christians and Muslims believe that there may come a time when we exist again. As explained above, the common belief prevalent in these religions is that the soul lives on at death and on the Day of Judgement it may be reunited with its body or may exist in some new spiritual form. But although within the mainstream, it is believed we only have one life on earth, allusions to re-incarnation (being born again) are found within the mystical traditions of all three faiths.

It must be noted that there is a diversity of belief within each faith tradition and that the personal statements quoted here are the opinions of the particular individual and do not necessarily reflect the traditional teachings of the faith.

 Judaism

The Jewish View

> *The Lord gives and the Lord takes away. Blessed be the Lord.*

Book of Job, 1: 21

According to Judaism, all people are born innocent and created free with the ability to choose between good and bad actions. The world in which people are placed is a good world, created by God for the benefit of human beings. Jewish people have a responsibility to use their gifts to improve the world for other people. The good that people do live after them in the next generation.

> *I don't know if I'll exist when my body dies. I don't know what's going to happen to me when I die . . . the body perishes – ashes to ashes, dust to dust. What happens to the thing we call the soul is a very individual thought. My feeling is that it doesn't get lost. But I think it mainly goes through to the next generation. What I do, what I think, what they think about me, all that encompasses something which they carry on . . . It may be in their minds, it may be in their hearts. They will talk to their children. Something of what I say, or what I believe in, I think will be passed on. And possibly that may be the main thing that happens. It may be that somewhere in a world unknown there is the people's spirit whatever that is . . . it's gathered together, and maybe it is something which feeds the future generation; but this is hidden from us. This is something which nobody can tell.*

Paul

Although Jewish people pay far more attention to living life here and now than preparing for the life to come, there are many discussions in the Talmud about a Day of Judgement and some people do think and talk about it:

> *What will happen to me? Well, I suppose I'll disintegrate bodily . . . bound to: but we believe that the soul leaves the body, and we believe that there's judgement after death . . . that you are called or summoned, to a court, a celestial court; and you are judged on all your doings throughout the years that you were alive, and you are either rewarded or punished accordingly.*
>
> Alan

It is on this Judgement Day that the resurrection of the dead takes place. The resurrection of the dead is an important principle in Jewish teaching but there is no one tradition as to the actual form this resurrection will take. Some scholars have spoken of a bodily resurrection whilst others such as Maimonides (1135–1204) of a spiritual resurrection. Maimonides pointed out the difficulties of a physical resurrection because inevitably the resurrected body will die again and therefore Maimonides says the soul alone will enjoy immortality.

According to Jewish Tradition, the resurrection of the dead takes place when the Messiah appears in the world. The Messiah is described in the Biblical Book of Isaiah as being a descendent of King David. And it is the Messiah who is the forerunner of the messianic age when there will be peace and harmony for all humanity throughout the world.

When someone dies friends and community can help so much. Within Judaism, there is a tradition of 'shiva' – a period of seven days when the home of the deceased is open for friends and family. Special prayers are said and people bring food for the chief mourners.

> *I lost one of my best friends about two years ago. It was just such a hard time . . . I felt she'd left this huge gap in my life . . . it was so good to have my friends around . . . people I had met through the Jewish community who were all going through the same thing. It was nice that we'd go together to the shiva house in the evening and although it wasn't in our town everyone made sure we could all get to it . . . and we'd speak to her parents and tell them how much she meant to us. It was a time to talk which I found so helpful and then a year later when it was time for the stone setting (memorial stone placed on grave) we were able to re-gather our thoughts. Now it wasn't just crying we'd all been through a year of experience and we'd learnt to cope with the fact that there was a gap in our group of friends. But it was nice to have that community feeling that we are all close and like a family. It's hard to lose a friend but she was so ill and she took the positives out of life and I think I definitely learnt a lot more to live each day to the full as much as you can and not have a go when things go wrong but just pick yourself up.*
>
> Eva

 *Christianity*

The Christian View

> *Jesus said: He who believes in me will live, even though he dies.*
>
> John 11: 25

There are different opinions as to what happens to us after death depending on the particular Christian denomination, but all Christians believe that Christ Himself rose from the dead and that those who believe in him also have hope of a life beyond death (1 Corinthians, 15: 20–1). Roman

Catholics teach that only those who put their trust in Christ and who have led a really pure life will enter Heaven and be in God's presence immediately. The majority have to undergo a period of purification called Purgatory, where their chief suffering will be their great distance from God. But with the help of the prayers of the living, the saying of masses and the help of the saints, their souls will at last be cleansed of all sin and they will see God. Many Roman Catholics believe that those who die loving evil and hating God will suffer in Hell. One day Jesus will come in final judgement and the dead will rise and the universe be cleansed and changed.

Although not all Christians would agree with this view, most would agree with the words in the Nicene Creed – one of the earliest statements of Christian doctrine, 'I look for the resurrection of the dead and the life of the world to come', but they do not define what that means. Protestants tend to emphasise that our physical bodies are mortal and that it is a person's soul that is everlasting and that those who put their faith in Christ's sacrificial love can be saved from the consequences of sin and inherit eternal life in heaven.

Christianity proclaims that the end is already here in that God has entered the world in the form of Jesus, (New Testament, John 1: 1–14) and that Jesus Christ has saved us from our sins by his death and resurrection. Those who believe in him have eternal life already. And when they die, their souls will be at one with God and when Jesus comes again they will be raised to a new life.

> Now that I've accepted Jesus Christ, I look on death as a sleep . . . that's to say, a passing from death into life: and death is just a rest for a while, until Jesus Christ himself shall come back and claim his people. In the meantime, I'd like to think I will go to heaven, though perhaps I'll have to go to purgatory first. I hope I'll go to heaven: heaven to my mind is perfect peace . . . that's the only way I can describe it.
>
> Julie

Christians believe that at the second coming of Jesus there will be a final judgement and the conclusion of creation (Matthew 24: 29–31).

> When Jesus comes again the good ones will be taken with him into paradise . . . it'll be the best of everything – even better than heaven – the world as we know it won't exist any more . . . this will be a new world . . . I know it sounds very far-fetched and space-agey. They also say it's the Day of Judgement and then you're judged on your past life and it's almost like picking people out like OK and saying you did this so you go this way and you did that so you go that way.
>
> Pozza

What form that resurrection will actually take is not clear. However, one thing all Christians are agreed upon, and that is that a person has only one life on earth and that there are no second chances available in future lives here. This gives a sense of urgency to many who preach that one must decide to put one's faith in Christ before it is too late. No one can know when death will come.

 Islam

The Muslim View

> It is Allah who has given you life, and He who will cause you to die and make you live again.
>
> Qur'an: 2: 28

Many Muslims believe that this life is a test in preparation for the next world. After death there is a Day of Judgement. The bodies of the dead remain in their graves until this day when God will judge both Muslims and non-Muslims. On the Day of Judgement everyone will appear before God and will be assigned to paradise or to hell depending on whether a person's actions have been mainly good or mainly bad. The Qur'an gives clear descriptions of the Day of Judgement: paradise is pictured as a beautiful garden and hell, as a place of fire and torment:

> *When the earth shakes and quivers and the mountains crumble away and scatter abroad into fine dust, you shall be divided into three multitudes: those on the right (blessed shall be those on the right); those on the left (damned shall be those on the left); and those to the fore (foremost shall be those). Such are they that shall be brought near to their Lord in the gardens of delight . . . They shall recline on jewelled couches face to face, and there shall wait on them immortal youths with bowls and ewers and a cup of purest wine . . . As for those on the left hand . . . they shall dwell amidst scorching winds and boiling water.*

> Qur'an: 56: 4–42

At the time of death, the soul is extracted from the body and taken towards heaven and then returned back to its respective body and grave. On its return, the angels will ask three questions: Who is your God? What is your faith? Who is your prophet? The degree of comfort offered by the grave varies according to the answers to these questions.

> *We bury the body as soon as possible . . . the soul is taken . . . we respect the body . . . the soul travels until the Day of Judgement when we will all be resurrected and we all will be judged . . . you will know instinctively where the soul is going . . . if you were a good person than your grave will be expanded and it will be comfortable for you and you will smell nice and you will be treated well in the grave but if you had not lived your . . . life in a good way and had not practised your faith your punishment will start in the grave . . . your grave will be heavily constricted. They say to pray for protection from the grave . . . when you want to be granted paradise you are also asked to pray to be saved from the punishment of the grave because there are many, many prophets including Muhammad who have described the punishment of the grave.*

> Anisa

Eastern Salvationist or Mystical Tradition

 Hinduism

The Hindu View

> *As a man changes his clothes so the spirit changes its bodies.*

> Bhagavad Gita: 2. 22

Many Hindus believe that we have lived before in another life and that when we die we are born again in a new form – perhaps as another person, as an animal or as an insect. It is the atma – soul that is re-born many, many times, until it becomes one with God. Atma – soul is another way of saying the life force that is in every person, animal and plant. If we have lived a good life, we will be born again in a higher, more perfect form. And if we have lived a bad life we will be born again in a lower, less perfect form. How many times the atma is re-born is determined by karma – on how a person behaves in this world. No English translation does justice to the Sanskrit word karma, although clichés such as 'as you sow, so shall you reap' and 'what goes around, comes around' give some sense of karmic law. The law of karma traditionally leads on to the classification of human beings into strict classes or castes.

The caste system was originally based on the economic concept of division of labour. The Brahmins – the highest caste – were scholars who performed the important rites at the time of birth, marriage and death. The Kshatriyas were the warriors who were in charge of defending the country from outside invaders. The Vaishyas were the trades or business people and the Sudras were the working class. Later the high castes started to exploit the lower classes by depriving them of education and started to call them 'untouchables'. Mahatma Gandhi (1869–1948) called them Harijams – children of God and tried to eradicate these divisions. Today in India and all over the world the caste system among Hindus is gradually disappearing.

According to Hinduism, whatever good or bad we do in this life helps the soul to transmigrate – to detach from its body at death and attach itself to another human, animal or vegetable body. For many Hindus, the world is seen as the training ground for the soul. The training is complete when the soul finds its real self and becomes part of God and so obtains moksha – release from transmigration – the soul re-attaching itself to another living form.

> *As our religion says, death will only be the end of my physical life. But we don't walk around worrying about re-birth. We try to do the best we can according to our place in the family and society and hope that we will be re-born to a better existence. But It depends on Almighty God where he sends my soul – and I might come in another shape. If you believe, as I do, that there is one God, and every human being is a part of that God, then being part of God is being part of one great family; and just as, in a family, if you have children who are naughty, you have to punish them . . . and if they have been good and they have adapted to what you want them to do, then you reward them . . . being born again is like that.*

Anjeet

 Sikhism

The Sikh view

> *Those who die in thoughts of God are liberated from the cycle of life and death and the Lord shall abide in their hearts.*

The Guru Granth Sahib, 526

Most Sikhs believe that God controls what happens to every living plant and creature after they die. According to Sikhism, the human creature is made up of a body and soul. The body belongs to the physical world where it is born and dies but the soul belongs to the spiritual world that is God. The spiritual universe is as vast and infinite as the physical one. Sikhs believe that a person will be reincarnated again and again until their soul is united with God. A person's soul, being a minute part of the Eternal Soul that is the one God, has existed from the time of creation.

In the Guru Granth Sahib – the holy scriptures – the Gurus revealed that there are 8,400,000 living forms in the universe, half on land and half in the water. A human being is the supreme form of living and it is in this form that we have been given the choice to achieve oneness with God. The soul passes through all stages of existence from the soul of an insect to the soul of a human being. Until the time it is re-absorbed into God, the soul remains separate and is able to transmigrate:

> *According to the Sikh belief, the soul never dies – the soul persists even when the body is gone. And we also believe that whatever good or bad I did in this life, it leaves a sort of impression on my soul: whatever good or bad I do in this life is imprinted, as it were, on the soul, and this lasts with the soul. The soul will have the same tendency to steal if I'm a thief in this life; and it*

*will have a tendency to accumulate wealth if I'm doing it now. When I take the next birth, all
these tendencies will still persist.*

Pardeep

Sikhs believe that only through Nam Jupna – meditation, Kirath Kurna – earning an honest living and
Wond Chakna – sharing your earnings with the needy is it possible to achieve union with God during
this lifetime.

 Buddhism

The Buddhist View

> *All things that exist are subject to decay.*

Sabbe sankhara anicca, Dhammapada 277

Buddhists believe that at the time of death our stream of consciousness does not cease but continues
into a new re-birth usually dependent upon the kind of life we have led and the quality of our mind.
Our consciousness can survive in many forms and places: in animals and in the various planets as well
as in human beings in this world.

For Buddhists, it is in one sense misleading to talk of reincarnation – re-birth, because that suggests
that there is a 'something' – a self or soul – to be re-born. It may also suggest that the soul is part
of God. Buddhism does not refer specifically to God although some followers believe in God as well
as the teachings of Buddhism.

The founder of Buddhism, Siddhartha Gautama is called The Buddha (sometimes known as
Gautama Buddha) – literally The Enlightened One. The Buddha said that a person is made up of an
ever-changing, perishable 'body' and even faster changing mind. The body and mind complex is
further divided into five components called the khandhas: physical features, feeling, awareness of
senses, intentions and thinking powers. All of these are constantly changing. For example, the
khandhas of an adult are very different from the khandhas of a baby because an adult looks and
thinks differently. In fact the khandas are in a constant flux, changing all the time, moment to
moment. Our bodies although appearing the same day to day, will change several times over a 24
hour period. None of the atoms stay still. Decay and regeneration takes place continuously and
without a break. The same goes for the 'mind' khandas. Thoughts, feelings, awareness of senses and
intentions change ever more rapidly. The khandhas dissolve when a person dies. They are not carried
on to the next life. What is carried on is karma – the strong craving that we have within us to want
things and be selfish.

The Buddha said we break the effects of karma by giving up personal desires, which leads to
nirvana – spiritual freedom from space and time, from delusion and from passion. Since there is no
craving, there will be nothing left to be born again and the person will become an arahat – an
enlightened person. Enlightenment should not be taken as the end of life. Arahathood is mostly
attained while living. The arahats constantly live in the ever-changing present moment. All Buddhists
are encouraged to live this way. Learning form past mistakes is excellent but regretting is not.
Planning for the future is acceptable but not with attachment and rigidity.

> *I think when I die there'll just be a sense of presence that my teacher and Buddha are with me.
> I don't know what will happen to me after that. It depends on my karma.*

Tenzin Chozom

Chapter 7

What do I Believe?

When we have thought about and are comfortable with our own values and beliefs, we are more likely to be able to encourage others to think about their personal values and underlying beliefs. This chapter looks at personal beliefs, beliefs that focus on social issues and secular philosophical and religious beliefs. It questions the influences on what we believe and how our beliefs affect the way we see the world. Young people from within secular and religious communities give their views and throughout the chapter there are 'Stop and Think' points for you and your colleagues. At the end of the chapter, there are two activities designed to encourage young people to think about personal belief.

What is belief?

Believing is about knowing something is true. It's easy to believe in some things. Nobody is going to deny a fact like a triangle has three sides. This is an objective truth: a rational belief uncoloured by feeling or opinion. The chart below distinguishes some of the different kinds of beliefs that this chapter examines.

Fact belief	Belief that triangle has three sides.
Issue belief	Belief that human cloning is right.
Personal belief	Belief about ourselves.
Secular philosophical belief	Belief in a system for a way of life.
Religious belief	Belief in some or all of the teachings of a religion that cannot be proved beyond reasonable doubt.

Belief chart

Issue belief

There are beliefs to do with particular issues where truth is subjective and dependent upon a particular point of view. Issues like blood sports, climate change and human cloning where we need to make up our own mind. For example, in the case of human cloning, some people believe that it is right to use human stem cells for medical research in order to advance the treatment of spinal cord injuries, cancer, diabetes and degenerative diseases like Parkinson's and Alzheimer's. Superman star, Christopher Reeve who died in 2004 passionately believed in stem cell research in the hope that it might eventually provide a cure for paralysis. Other people are adamantly against human cloning arguing that stem cells are potential human beings and using them as laboratory material may lead to a world in which copies of babies are made without two parents.

These are issues that it is possible to have an informed opinion about. Underlying these issues are far deeper questions about why we think the way we do and why we believe what we believe. Knowing more about what we really think probably means questioning ourselves about our experiences and the past influences on our lives. Thinking through our personal philosophy helps us to recognise and respond to the experiences of other people. In dealing with adolescence, we are often coping with periods of introspection and acute changes in attitudes and opinions. Being prepared helps a lot.

Activity: you/colleagues/young people

- Finish these sentences:
  - The issue I believe most important is . . .
  - I would stand up and be counted for the particular cause of . . .
  - I feel sure that . . .
  - I agree with the idea of . . .
- Identify two things you believe are wrong and two you believe are right and for each put forward a supporting argument.
- Describe two different things that other people feel are right and wrong and for each put forward a supporting argument.

Personal belief

There are four major factors that influence what we believe about ourselves:

- personality
- experience
- environment
- upbringing

Personality

Individual personality is a dominant influence on personal belief. Personality has been defined in various ways but some of its main components are intuition, imagination, emotion, rationality, intellect and humour. Within each unique personality there are specific traits; some people are naturally shy whilst others are extrovert, some people are easily excitable while others are placid, etc. etc. Insight into our own particular personality helps us to understand why we see the world the way we do and why the things we believe in are not necessarily the same things that other people believe in:

> *I once went to a happy-clappy church group service. It was very noisy, people were dancing . . . everyone was introducing themselves and chatting away. Quite frankly, it put me off completely. But looking back on the experience, I think I was put off because I'm a shy person and don't feel comfortable with loads of people around me.*
>
> Serena

Personality psychology tries to make sense of human behaviour, to discover the uniformities of character among individuals and to devise general principles in order to explain particular motives. There is always a danger that personality theories are used to stereotype and make quick judgements that are not necessarily accurate. There are many theories and each theory is only one interpretation of the human personality. Here is an outline of the Type and Trait personality theories.

Type theories

Long ago, before the days of psychology, Hippocrates and Galen in ancient Greece wrote of personality types. According to their theory, individual personalities can be classified into four temperaments on the basis of the dominance of one of four body fluids – lymph, yellow bile, black bile and blood corresponding to a personality that is mainly phlegmatic/apathetic and sluggish, choleric/angry, melancholic/depressed and gloomy and sanguine/confident and happy.

The Austrian psychiatrist Alfred Adler (1870–1937) relates to this early temperament theory in his work. Adler developed his scheme of personality types based on the degree of social interest and activity level in different personalities. His four personality types were:

1. The ruling-dominant type (choleric) – this person is assertive, aggressive and active. They manipulate and master life events and situations and have high activity levels and low social interest levels.
2. The getting-leaning type (phlegmatic) – this person expects others to satisfy their needs and to provide for their interests and has a low activity level and a low social interest level.
3. The avoiding type (melancholic) – this person is inclined to achieve success by circumventing a problem or withdrawing from it and has a low activity level and a low social interest level.
4. The socially useful type (sanguine) – this person is said to be the healthiest of all. The socially useful person attacks problems head on, is socially oriented and is prepared to co-operate with others.

Other psychologists who use type theories include the Swiss psychiatrist and psychoanalyst, Carl Gustav Jung (1875–1961) and the American psychologist, William H. Sheldon (1898–1970).

Trait theories

All trait theories assume that one's personality is a mixture of traits, i.e. permanent characteristic ways of behaving, thinking, feeling, reacting, etc. The early trait theories were little more than lists of adjectives. The British-born American psychologist Raymond B. Cattell (born 1905) based his influential theory on a set of deep source traits which are the 'real structural influences underlying personality' (Reber, 2001: 525).

Many personality psychologists present five traits as the crucial dimensions that govern personality. These are Neuroticism (sometimes labelled 'Emotional Stability'), Extroversion, Openness to Experience (sometimes labelled 'Intellect'), Agreeableness and Conscientiousness. (www.personalityresearch.org/bigfive/costa.html)

Neuroticism

The general tendency to experience negative feelings such as fear, sadness, embarrassment, anger, guilt and disgust is the core of neuroticism. Individuals high in neuroticism are also prone to have irrational ideas, to be less able to control their impulses and to cope more poorly than others with stress. Individuals low in neuroticism display characteristics of emotional stability and are even-tempered, relaxed and face stressful situations without being upset and rattled.

Extroversion

The German-born British psychologist Hans Jurgen Eysenck (1916–94) coined the term 'extroversion' in 1947. Extroverts are sociable, assertive, active and talkative. They like excitement and stimulation and tend to be cheerful, upbeat, energetic and optimistic. Salespeople represent the prototypic extroverts in our culture (Costa and McCrae, 1984: 141–57).

Introverts are less easy to define. In some respects, introversion can be seen as the absence of extroversion rather than what might be assumed to be its opposite. Introverts are reserved rather than unfriendly, independent rather than followers and even-paced rather than sluggish. Introverts may say they are shy when they mean that they prefer to be alone. They do not necessarily suffer from anxiety in the company of others. And although they may not have the same exuberant high spirits as extroverts, introverts are not necessarily unhappy or pessimistic (Costa and McCrae, 1980: 668–78).

Openness to experience

Open individuals are curious about both inner and outer worlds and their lives are rich in experiences. Characteristics are active imagination, sensitivity, a wide range of interests, intellectual curiosity and independence of judgement. Such people are willing to entertain new ideas and unconventional values and experience both positive and negative emotions more keenly than do closed individuals.

Openness is especially related to certain aspects of intelligence, such as divergent thinking, that contribute to creativity. But openness is not equivalent to intelligence. Some very intelligent people are wholly disinterested in new experiences, and some very open people are quite limited in intellectual capacity.

People who are low on openness to experience tend to be conventional in behaviour and conservative in outlook. They prefer the familiar to the novel and their emotional responses are somewhat muted. Closed people generally have a narrower scope and intensity of interests. Although they tend to be socially and politically conservative, closed people should not be viewed as authoritarians. Closedness does not suggest aggressive intolerance or hostility. Such qualities are more likely to be signs of extremely low agreeableness.

Agreeableness

The agreeable person is fundamentally unselfish. They are sympathetic to others and eager to help them and believe that others will be equally helpful in return. By contrast, the disagreeable or antagonistic person is egocentric, sceptical of others and competitive rather than co-operative.

Conscientiousness

Conscientious individuals are purposeful, strong-willed and determined. Jack Digman (1923–98) and his student Takemoto-Chock (www.personalityresearch.org/bigfive/jack.html) refer to this factor as the Will to Achieve. On the positive side, a high level of conscientiousness is associated with punctuality, reliability and achievement. On the negative side, it may lead to annoying fastidiousness, compulsive neatness and workaholic behaviour.

People with low levels of conscientiousness are not necessarily lacking in moral principles, but such individuals may be less exacting in applying them, just as they are more lackadaisical in working toward their goals.

You may want to explore this topic of personality psychology further. Isabel Myers and Katherine Cook Briggs (www.myersbrigs.com) and Meridith Belbin (www.belbin.com) have written about personalities in a team; how people prefer to focus their attention, how they take in information, make decisions and relate to the outside world. Both organisations provide tests to ascertain personality type.

Experience

Just as personality is a major factor in what we believe about ourselves, so too is our unique experience of life. External events that stand out in our lives and the experience of joyful and sad moments help shape personal philosophy:

> *After my dad died, it was impossible for me to believe in a god . . . I just thought that no god would let a person die the way I saw him die . . . it just wasn't on . . . I stopped praying completely.*
>
> Sanjeev

Other individuals may experience exactly the same situation as Sanjeev but respond in a completely different way. How we shape our personal philosophy in the light of experience depends upon an inter-play of personality, environment and upbringing. So even within a specific culture or faith tradition, it is unlikely that two individuals experiencing the same environment and upbringing will have exactly the same value and belief system.

Austrian psychoanalyst Sigmund Freud (1856–1939) thought that a belief system that involves an organised religion stems from the experience of having been a helpless baby totally dependent on its parents/carers. The infant perceives its carers as all-powerful beings who show it great love and satisfy all its needs. As we grow older, Freud suggested that we transfer this dependency on to religion. Freud also suggested that many childhood experiences cause people to have very complex feelings about their primary carers and themselves, and religion and religious rituals provide an existing mechanism for working these out (www.bbc.co.uk/religion/atheism)

Environment

The environment we live in has a strong influence on what we believe. Whether we live in a developing country, a western industrialised country, a theocracy or democracy, the rulers have the power to influence our beliefs. For example, someone raised in Communist China is unlikely to have a belief in God. Rarely if ever, have they met a believer, and the education system and peer pressure from the people they meet make being an atheist the natural thing to do.

On a more parochial level, the local environment affects our world-view. We may live in a remote, small village or in a vibrant multi-cultural city. On where we live depends upon what opportunities we have for meeting people, work and leisure experiences. And on these opportunities depends the influence of friends, peer-group and the media.

Upbringing

The people who look after us when we are young have a profound influence on our personal beliefs:

> *I hated the way I was brought up . . . it was a lot of hocus-pocus . . . rules stuffed down my throat . . . we were told they came from God but I know they are man-made and they don't mean anything to me . . . I can be just as much a good person without any of that stuff.*
>
> Answer

Some people adopt the beliefs of their family, others reject some or all of them and others reject and return to them later:

> *We sometimes talked about what we believed when I was growing up . . . I suppose I go up and down in my belief level . . . sometimes I've thought that there might be some sort of power*

greater than people and sometimes I'm not so sure but now I've got a baby I do think about the miracle of it all . . . how this little boy came to be and it makes me wonder.

Shelley

Stop and Think: you/colleagues

- How did you acquire your beliefs?
- Has your personality, experience, environment and upbringing affected your beliefs?
- How?
- Which one of these four factors is most influential?
- Which one of these four factors is least influential?
- How do your beliefs influence your behaviour?

Secular philosophical belief

Looking at what secular as well as religious philosophers have to say is helpful in developing an understanding of what other people believe at the same time as thinking about what we ourselves believe.

Philosophy – 'love of wisdom and knowledge' (*Oxford Dictionary*, 1964: 912) – is a very broad term with many meanings (Angeles, 1992: 227). Within the context of this book, philosophy is perhaps best expressed as a means by which we can ask questions in order to think more deeply about our lives and the lives of people around us. Here is an outline of three secular philosophies: atheism, agnosticism and humanism.

Atheism

Atheism is a philosophical term literally meaning, *atheos*, Greek for 'without God' (1964: 72). It is the belief that gods do not, or God does not exist. It is also the personal lack of belief in a particular God. Is it possible to be both religious and an atheist? It looks like it is possible because, for example, the ancient eastern religion of Buddhism (see below) does not believe in gods or the One God, yet the followers of Buddhism consider they belong to a religion.

The classical Greek philosophers did not go as far as the followers of Buddhism. They never categorically denied the existence of gods or the One God but there were several philosophers including Protagorus (about 485–420 BCE) from the Sophist School of Philosophy who placed human beings above the One God.

Famous atheists include Ludwig Feuerbach, the 19th century German philosopher who said that our ideas about God were merely the projection of our ideas about human beings onto an imaginary supernatural being. So we transfer to this imaginary supernatural being the control, power, love and goodness that we really want to possess ourselves. The French sociologist, Emile Durkheim (1858–1917) took another view. He thought that religion was produced by human society, and had nothing supernatural about it: 'Religious force is nothing other than the collective and anonymous force of the clan' (www.bbc.co.uk/religion/atheism).

Nowadays there are many types of atheism. Secularism is an atheist philosophy that emphasises that nobody should be disadvantaged for not having a religious faith. Christian Non-Realism is a form of Christianity, which does without an external God. Postmodernism is a view of religion without

God, and without any absolute values and Humanism (see below) is a philosophy of life that understands the world without incorporating the supernatural.

Agnosticism

Agnosticism is the philosophical term for the belief that we cannot have knowledge of God and that it is impossible to prove that God exists or does not exist (Angeles, 1993: 6). It is difficult to say who founded agnosticism; probably these ideas have been around since human beings began to think about the natural world and where they came from. We know from the writings of the ancient Greek philosophers that some people such as Epicurus (see section on 'Humanism') were agnostic yet the term 'agnostic' was not coined until the 1840s. The British philosopher and theologian, Thomas Huxley (1825–95) combined the letter, 'a' which implies the negative with 'gnostic' the Greek word for knowledge so meaning literally 'no knowledge'.

Famous agnostics include the geologist and writer, Charles Darwin (1809-1885). He wrote in his book *Life and Letters* about his personal beliefs: 'I think an Agnostic would be the more correct description of my state of mind. The whole subject (of God) is beyond the scope of man's intellect'. (www.religioustolerance.org)

Humanism

Many people who are atheist or agnostics are humanists. Humanism is a way of looking at the world that focusses on human beings and not on God: 'a system concerned with human (not divine) interests' (*The Concise Oxford English Dictionary*, 1964: 591). The term humanism was adopted in the 19th century at the time of the French Enlightenment.

How and by whom founded

The British Humanist Association traces many of its ideas back to ancient times. Before Common Era (BCE), i.e. before the time of Jesus Christ (BC) some of the classical Greek philosophers made sense of life without depending on a supernatural power such as God. Protagoras (490–421 BCE) explored morality and stated 'man is the measure of all things' and Epicurus (341–270 BCE) argued that the principle for good and evil is human consciousness.

Later during the Roman Period, the Latin poet Lucretius (about 55 BCE) wrote *On The Nature of Things* which put forward the theory of Epicurus that the human soul is material and dies with the body. Ideas of human-centred morality can also be traced back to the ancient civilisations of China and India.

During the European Renaissance (14th–16th century), scholars, at times called humanists, rediscovered ancient knowledge and began to explore the natural world with science. The Polish astronomer, Nicolaus Copernicus (1473–1543) in his book *The Revolutions of the Celestial Spheres* overturned the view that the earth is at the centre of the universe. Copernicus proved scientifically that the planets – including the Earth – revolve round the sun. This implied that everything can be scientifically tested; that rather than living by faith, people can examine the facts of the world and their place in it. This was very challenging to the authority of the Catholic Church, which banned Copernicus's book until 1835 (www.channel4.com/believeitornot).

The 18th century French Enlightenment philosophers such as Voltaire (1694–1778) challenged superstition, intolerance, dogma and injustice by arguing that human reason is the best guide to all knowledge and human concerns. Within 50 years of the Enlightenment, the British Utilitarian philosophers Jeremy Bentham (1748–1832) and John Stuart Mill (1806–73) suggested that moral laws should enable the greatest happiness to be given to the greatest number of people. At about the same time, Charles Darwin's Theory of Evolution (1859) shook the world by showing how humans could have evolved naturally from simple creatures like the monkey.

In 1866 the National Secular Society was formed to encourage freethinking and in 1899 the Rationalist Press Association was founded under Charles Albert Watts to publish 'free thought' books. In the 20th century, three years after the United Nations (UN) was formed, the UN General Assembly adopted the Universal Declaration of Human Rights (1948) detailing individual and social rights and freedoms. In 1953, the structure of DNA, the basic genetic building block of life was discovered. Ten years later in 1963, the British Humanist Association was founded from the earlier Ethical Union with Sir Julian Huxley as its first president (www.humanism.org.uk).

What followers believe

The basic belief of humanists begins with the assumption that not everybody accepts religious faith. Instead, humanism relies on scientific testing, reasoning and discussion to arrive at facts.

Most humanists believe that it is the overall quality of life that is important. They consider that all people have natural attributes of understanding, caring and cooperation, and an awareness of the consequences of their actions. Humanists believe that it is these characteristics that give us the urge to help each other, and to judge what actions will make life better for everyone.

Humanists follow a 'golden rule': 'Treat other people as you would like them to treat you.' This same precept is shared by all the world's religious faiths. Humanists have no other rules. There are still many mysteries in the universe and in life, so humanism is open to new evidence as and when it comes along. Humanists share common views on moral issues, but try to consider every possible consequence when discussing policies for action. The humanist beliefs in birth control and abortion rights, equal rights for everyone, voluntary euthanasia and freedom of speech have all been thrashed out in this way (www.humanism.org.uk).

> *I think it's great that the ideas I've come to myself are the same ideas that Humanists have come to. Things like tolerance and justice, and working out what is right for people even if it breaks an old-fashioned rule, and not destroying the environment because it's the only world we have.*
>
> Matt

Religious Belief

Religious belief is based on some or all of the teachings of a particular religious system. In religious terms, belief and faith go together. Religious people have faith or trust in a belief that cannot be proved one way or the other.

A key concept in many religions is belief in one or more higher beings that, as creators of the universe, have power over nature and the lives of people. These beings are often worshipped, and may be named deities or perceived as abstract sources of absolute power.

A vital part of many religions is a belief in the individual's spirit or soul as an entity that is distinct from the body and mind. This spirit is immortal and, after physical death, continues its existence either by reincarnation – being re-born within another living form as in the Eastern Salvationist/Mystical tradition or in an invisible spiritual world as in the Western Prophetic tradition where the spirit may be punished or rewarded for deeds that are performed during life.

Stop and Think: you/colleagues/young people

- How do we relate to people with different beliefs from our own?

Group Activity: you/colleagues/young people

Talk please

Invite colleagues, friends, carers or parents to speak about the everyday practice of their faith. Ask them about some of the beliefs and teachings behind their practice. Prepare questions for a follow-up question and answer session. For example, 'is joining your religion allowed?' and 'how does believing in your faith affect the way you think about and the way you behave to people who do not believe the same things as you do?'

Guide to religious belief

The world's major faiths roughly divide into two groups: the Western Prophetic tradition and the Salvationist or Eastern Mystical tradition. The Western tradition originated in the Near and Middle East and includes Judaism, Christianity and Islam. This tradition stresses the prophetic – God reveals his will to us through an agent: a prophet such as Moses in the Hebrew Bible and Muhammad in the Qur'an. The books in which these prophets appear are sacred and have authority over the lives of their readers.

The Eastern tradition began in India and includes Hinduism, Buddhism, Sikhism and their offshoots. The Eastern tradition stresses that God is found within the human spirit. Life on earth involves a mystical journey – a system that aims to achieve direct experience of God. It is a spiritual journey that has many stages on the way and may involve fasting, meditation and prayer.

The Eastern Mystical Tradition

 Hinduism

How and by whom founded

No one founder figure or single creed acknowledged. The word Hindu is a combination of two Sanskrit words – Hin = violence and Du = without – therefore Hindu literally means 'one without violence' and thus one who respects and preserves life. There is also no one sacred book but the Hindu scriptures include some of the world's oldest-known writings such as the Vedas. The Vedas describe Hindu worship and practice and were probably written down about 800 BCE but reflect an oral tradition from centuries before.

Language

Urdu, Hindi, Gujerati, Punjabi, and the language of the country of origin.

Main religious festivals

Dussehra – takes place in October and commemorates the time when Lord Rama fought with King Ravana and was victorious. Celebrations take place over ten days, during which the story of Ramayana is dramatically enacted. On the tenth day, an image of King Ravana is burned.

Diwali – the Festival of Lights takes place in November and marks the Lord Rama's safe return from exile. Special lights and candles are displayed in homes and public buildings and fire works are let off.

Holi – takes place in March and is a festival of colour.

Holy day

No one specific day of the week.

What followers believe

Hindus believe in one God, called Brahma who is known by many different names and appears in many different forms. For many Hindus the whole world, including the people in it, is a kind of reflection or manifestation of Brahma. There is no separation between Brahma and the world. In reality all these many different things are part of the one Brahma. Hindus believe we cannot really describe Brahma because it is much greater and more perfect than the many limited and imperfect forms through which it is expressed.

Apart from Brahma the most important thing for Hindus is the atma – self. Hindus believe that when we look deeply into ourselves we discover our real self, which lies behind the self that we show to other people. In fact some Hindus believe that this deep self is the same as Brahma, so that if we know our true self we know Brahma. This is called self-realisation.

Most Hindus believe in reincarnation – that we have lived before in another life and that when we die, our spirit is reborn in another form – perhaps as a person, as an animal or as an insect. If we have lived a good life, we will be born again in a higher, more perfect form. If we have lived a bad life then we will be born again in a lower, less perfect form. Ultimately, people who are eventually perfect finally escape the series of re-births and become at one with Brahma. This is the concept known as moksha – freedom from re-birth.

Traditionally, many Hindus believed that we are born into one of four castes or classes: the Brahmin or priest class, the warrior class, the farmer and artisan class and the labouring class. Each caste or social grouping has its own special religious duties and rites and prayers known as dharma – individual and social code of conduct. Dharma is the duty of every individual to act in the right way according to caste or social grouping, gender and age. Today in India and all over the world, the caste system among Hindus is gradually disappearing and in its place, we can see more and more equality among all classes.

However, individuals are still expected to act according to their stage of life. Human life is divided into four ashrams – stages. Approximately, the first 25 years – brahmcharya ashram are for learning and celibacy; the next 25 years – grahasth ashram are for marriage, family life and earning an honest living; the next 25 years – vanaprastha – for gradually detaching from the world of work and looking after family and a time to do community work to pay back to society and the final stage – sanyasa – for preparation for the next life so total surrender to God and renunciation of this world is called for.

The law of karma – actions – maintains that we get a position in life as a result of how good or badly we behaved in previous lives. Our present condition, our happiness and status are directly the result of our previous life. Consequently we are wholly responsible for our life now and our future. Karma is thus the moral law of cause and effect. It explains the inequalities of life as the consequences of actions in previous lives.

I like my religion because it does not seem boring in outlook. There is a lot of emphasis on enjoying life as much as possible, which I feel is important. It also discusses things, which other philosophies seem to shy away from, notably the idea of sex; there is quite a wealth of detail on this matter in the various tantric writings and in the Kama Sutra. This openness and frankness is highly appealing, and I find it a very practical guidance to living. I do however reject certain aspects of Hindu philosophy – I do not really believe in the idea of prayer, I feel that god is a higher consciousness of us, not something which can be prayed to in the real sense, but attained in unity. I also disagree with some of the archaic ideals of Hinduism, such as the forbidding of eating beef and the caste system, among other things.

Anish

 Buddhism

How and by whom founded

Siddhartha Gautama was an Indian prince born around 563 BCE in Lumbini in the foothills of the Himalayas. Determined to find the answer to the problems of sickness, old age and death, he gave up his kingdom and family and set off on a spiritual search that lasted for six years until he found the answer within himself. This is known as Enlightenment: the direct realisation of reality or how things truly are. Once Siddhartha Gautama became enlightened he was known as the Buddha or Awakened One.

The Buddha formulated the Ariya-Sacca – the Four Noble Truths:

1. All living things suffer
2. Suffering is originated by attachment
3. Cessation of suffering is possible/can be achieved
4. The Noble Eightfold Path leads to the ending of suffering

The Eightfold Path

1. Right understanding.
2. Right aspiration.
3. Right speech.
4. Right bodily action.
5. Right livelihood.
6. Right effort.
7. Right mindfulness.
8. Right concentration.

Language

Country of origin.

Main religious festivals

Different sects will have different days. Most sects celebrate the new year. The calendar is lunar so the festival dates vary from year to year.

Holy day

No one specific day of the week.

What followers believe

Buddhists believe that through meditation and self-discipline a person may gain the insightful wisdom and compassion to eventually become enlightened like the Buddha himself.

The basic Buddhist practice is shown by:

- ethical conduct
- meditation
- wisdom

Ethical conduct

This translates into Five Precepts that are intended to help us live in this world without causing harm to ourselves or others. These precepts follow the natural behaviour of an enlightened person. They are:

1. **Not to take life.** This means not killing any being down to an insect because everyone looks on their own life as very precious and does not want to suffer or die. So no being is ever harmed. In some Buddhist countries many people are vegetarians.

   Even as a mother protects with her life
   Her child, her only child,
   So with a boundless heart
   Should one cherish all living beings.

   (Karaniya) Metta Sutta, Suttanipata, 149 (Translation from the Pali.)
   Discourse on Loving-kindness

2. **Not to steal or take what is not given.** So respecting other's property just as we do not want others to steal anything belonging to us.
3. **Not committing sexual misconduct.** This means using our sexuality responsibly so that no one can be hurt by our actions.
4. **Not telling lies, slandering or gossiping.** In other words being careful of our speech to make sure it is honest, kind and helpful.
5. **Not indulging in alcohol or drugs** since these cause our mind to be out of control and cause endless problems in this world.

Meditation

There are many methods of meditation in the Buddhist world. But basically meditation is intended firstly to calm and concentrate the mind because a well-directed peaceful mind can lead to insight and wisdom. Buddhists train how to live in the present moment with a relaxed but clear mind, using a technique called mindfulness that focuses on the here and now, often using breathing as a base.

Wisdom

Wisdom is reached through ethical conduct and meditation. Meditation is practiced in order to have a calm and clear mind that goes beyond conceptual thinking: a mind that can directly experience our unborn natural awareness. This awareness is described as a luminous and blissful emptiness and in Mahayana Buddhism is sometimes called our Buddha Nature.

When we realise this awareness we spontaneously see that both ourselves and the outer world are not how we normally perceive them with our ignorant minds. Usually we experience the things around us and ourselves as solid and unchanging. There is no realisation of natural impermanence, of continual change moment to moment and of the lack of any inherent existence.

When we understand how our ordinary thinking patterns and emotions cause so much pain and problems not only for ourselves but also for others, then a sense of renunciation together with great compassion and loving kindness naturally arises in our hearts and we experience our inherent interconnection with all beings.

According to Buddhist belief, most of the events that we encounter in this life are a result of our past karma. The word karma literally means 'action'. Imagine that every intentional action of our body, speech and mind plants small seeds in our consciousness. And eventually, given the right causes and conditions, these seeds will ripen and we will experience the results of these actions sometime in the future. However since these causes were often created in former lifetimes it is difficult for us to understand the connection.

Nonetheless, the important point is not what caused the events that happen to us now, but how we can skilfully use whatever happens to us to create a good future. For instance, if we react with anger or greed, we are setting up patterns that will result in our future suffering whereas if we react with kindness and generosity we will bring good fortune into our future lives. Since this present lifetime is just a small section of the total picture, we should rejoice in our having attained a human birth and use it to benefit ourselves and others.

> *I am a Buddhist by choice and I have always been interested in a spiritual path having grown up in the Catholic faith and looked at various other religions over the years. I have attended a lot of teachings by various Tibetan Buddhist lamas – teachers. Tibetan Buddhism resonates with me . . . I feel at home in it although there are times when I have a lot of doubts about whether I really, really believe and question my faith. But despite the doubts, Buddhism gives me consolation and inspiration and a prescribed path to follow which can lead eventually to enlightenment in a future lifetime . . . I wouldn't dream of saying in this life time.*

Monica

 Sikhism

How and by whom founded

The word Sikh is derived from the Sanskrit word 'seekh' meaning 'to learn'. So the name implies one who learns or seeks the truth – a disciple.

Sikhism developed in the 15th century CE in an area called the Punjab – the land of the five rivers – Jehlum, Ravi, Chenab, Bias and Satluj – located between the Indus and Ganges Rivers. Historically, the name has been given to areas stretching from Afghanistan to Delhi. Now the name Punjab is used for one province in Pakistan and one state in India.

Founded by a man called Guru – spiritual teacher – Nanak (1469–1538 CE) who was born in the village of Talwandi near Lahore. Guru Nanak wanted his followers to continue his teachings after he died so he appointed a successor to carry on the teachings. In all there were ten Sikh gurus who, by the practical example of their own lives, showed the importance of Guru Nanak's teachings.

In 1603 the fifth guru, Guru Arjan began to compile his own writings as well as the writings of the first four gurus. The tenth guru, Guru Gobind Singh, added the writings of his father, the ninth guru, Guru Tegh Bahadur and named the book the Guru Granth Sahib. In 1699, Guru Gobind Singh said there would be no more living gurus and asked his followers to regard the Guru Granth Sahib as their everlasting guru.

The Guru Granth Sahib contains 1,430 pages and as well as the writings of the first five and the ninth guru, there are compositions from 30 bhagats – saints from both Hindu and Muslim backgrounds. The Guru Granth Sahib is honoured in the same way as a human guru would be and there are many respectful practices involved in reading from it. When Sikhs bow to the Guru Granth Sahib they are not only paying respect to the Sikh gurus but also to the holy ones of other faiths whose compositions are in the Guru Granth Sahib.

Language

Mainly Punjabi.

Main Religious Festivals

Vaisakhi – is New Year's Day in the Punjab and falls on the 13 April. The date is based on the solar calendar and is fixed, but once every 36 years it occurs on the 14 April. It is the time when Sikhs of adolescent age or older can choose to be initiated in to the Khalsa.

Diwali – is the festival of lights. It is held at the start of winter.

Guru Nanak's Birthday – the anniversary of the birth of the first guru. The date usually falls in November.

Holy day

No specific day of the week.

What followers believe

Sikhs believe in the one God and in the teachings of the Guru Granth Sahib. Sikhs believe in the equality of all and do not believe in caste or social distinctions. As a practical example of this, every Sikh sits on the floor in the gurdwara – community centre and place of worship – and women and men participate equally. The tenth guru, Guru Gobind Singh gave all male Sikhs the name Singh – literally meaning 'lion' and all women Sikhs the name Kaur – literally meaning 'princess' in order to show that everyone is equal. Sikhs pray for God to bless everyone 'May all prosper according to Divine Will' (Sikh Daily Ardas – Prayer).

The Khalsa – literally 'pure ones' were created at an initiation ceremony by the tenth guru, Guru Gobind Singh on Vaisakhi Day – a festival of thanksgiving – in 1699. By this ceremony, he aimed to create a loyal world community with a strong identity. It took about 230 years (1469–1699) for the ten gurus to practically perform all the learning techniques of being God-centred humans and to become Khalsa (pure ones). Guru Gobind Singh asked all Sikhs to wear five symbols. As the words for all five signs begin with the letter 'K', the signs are often called the Five Ks: kesh – uncut hair symbolising the gift of hair to human beings, kangha – comb worn to tie back the hair symbolising personal care and cleanliness, kara – steel bracelet symbolising responsibility and allegiance to God, katcha – shorts symbolising chastity and modesty and kirpan – a small dagger symbolising resistance against evil sometimes worn as an emblem on a chain around the neck (Bowker, 1997: 87). Sikhs celebrate the creation of Khalsa (pure ones) every April at the Vaisakhi festival.

> *I am a proud British Sikh. I believe everyone is equal in the eyes of God, no matter what gender, creed, culture, etc. I like the fact that under Sikhism there is no caste system and that everyone is equal. I believe everyone should not harm or upset anyone as we are all a family in a way under the eyes of God and are therefore brothers and sisters of God. I believe that if anyone wants to learn about how to be a good Sikh then this can be done by the teachings of the Sikh Holy Book, The Guru Granth Sahib. This contains stories and should be followed as it is the last existing evidence of Sikhism after the 10 Gurus.*

Nikki

The Western Prophetic Tradition

 Judaism

How and by whom founded

The early history of the Jewish people is told in the Hebrew Bible, in particular in the Pentateuch, known as the Five Books of Moses – the first five books of the Old Testament.

No single founder but the patriarchs Abraham, Isaac and Jacob and the matriarchs Sarah, Rebecca and Rachel are revered as the ancestors of the Jewish people. Abraham was the first known person to believe in the One God. He left a land full of idols in Mesopotamia in about 1800 BCE (Book of Genesis 12: 1–5) to settle in the land of Canaan – now known as Israel and Palestine. When famine came to Canaan, Abraham's grandson, Jacob and his 12 sons went to Egypt, where they were later made slaves to the King of Egypt. Then in about 1250 BCE their descendents, the Hebrews were led out of Egypt back to Canaan by Moses. On the way, at Mount Sinai Moses received God's Torah – the Written Law – that contains the Ten Commandments and is the basis of Jewish practice and belief today.

Language

In Israel, modern Hebrew and in other places the language of the country of origin.

Main religious festivals

Rosh Hashanah – the Jewish New Year celebrated in September/October.
Yom Kippur – the Day of Atonement, the holiest day of the year. It begins at sunset on the ninth day after Rosh Hashanah and is marked by 25 hours of prayer and fasting.
Pesach – the festival of Passover celebrated in the spring.
Shavout – the festival of Pentecost celebrated in May/June.
Sukkot – the festival of Tabernacles begins five days after *Yom Kippur* and continues for seven days.

Holy day

The Sabbath starts at Friday sunset and lasts until an hour after Saturday sunset.

What followers believe

Most Jewish people believe in the One God with no intermediary. Judaism is a way of practical everyday living rather than a rigid belief system. The way of life is regulated by the commandments given by God in the Torah – the written law – in conjunction with the enormous collection of commentaries and interpretations of oral law in the Talmud, completed in approximately 500 CE.

There is no creed as such but the medieval Jewish philosopher Moses Maimonides (1135–1204), drew up 13 articles of faith, which are generally considered to sum up the essentials of Jewish belief:

- The existence of the Creator.
- His unity.
- His incorporeality (God is not material).
- His eternity.
- The obligation to serve and worship Him alone.
- The existence of prophecy.
- The superiority of Moses to all the prophets.
- The revelation of the Law to Moses at Sinai.
- The unchanging nature of the Law.
- The omniscience of God (God is all-knowing).
- Retribution in this world and the next (recompense for evil or for good done).
- The coming of the Messiah.
- The resurrection of the dead – revival and restoration.

I think the thing that I really like about my religion is the family thing – even when you don't see your family all week there's always that Friday night or even on a religious holiday when you can sit down for a meal and talk. I don't think you'd necessarily have time otherwise . . . with my parents always busy at work. There's also the sense of community at my synagogue . . . I've got lots of friends there. But on the other hand, I also find it hard . . . some of my friends aren't religious and that can cause problems. Like when they all go out without me on a Saturday night and I find that quite hard because then I sometimes feel lonely and left out. And also having to keep kosher (dietary laws) . . . some people don't understand and sometimes it can be very difficult . . . there's nothing for me to eat and they just think I'm being fussy but other friends will be fine and will go and eat where I can eat or help me to find something I can eat . . . I think it's because we're all at different stages of observance as far as religion is concerned and that can be difficult.

Eva

 *Christianity*

How and by whom founded

Christianity is founded on faith in Jesus Christ as the one who came as the human Son and Man to show us what human life is meant to be like and who was also the divine Son of God showing us what God is like. His followers recognised Him as Jesus the Messiah (meaning 'anointed one') the One long expected in the Hebrew Scriptures. Jesus was born as the son of Mary and Joseph, a carpenter, in the town of Bethlehem that is in Israel and Palestine. He was born just before the death of Herod the Great, King of Judea in 4 BCE (Before Common Era or BC Before Christ). When he was about 30 years old he left his job as a carpenter and began to preach in synagogues and on the hillsides and became well known throughout the area as the teacher and healer. He called a group of 12 people to follow him and to carry on his work after he died. They became known as the Apostles.

During his life he continued to observe the Jewish tradition he had been born into but he gave different interpretations to some of the traditional teaching in the Hebrew Bible (Old Testament). He challenged the religious leaders of his time to show great sincerity in their adherence to and practice of the law. His own ministry was mainly centred on Galilee and Jerusalem but he had several encounters with Gentiles and he became convinced that his message of peace and love was meant to be taken to the whole world. So after his death and resurrection, he sent his followers out into all parts of the world.

After Jesus died his followers, particularly the Apostles – the first 12 people that Jesus instructed to preach – wrote down what they remembered of his preaching and his life. The stories about Jesus were collected into four books that are called Gospels – good news brought by Jesus. Some of the Apostles also wrote Epistles – letters – to the early Christian groups and these letters together with the Gospels are called the New Testament that forms the basis of Christian belief.

Language

Country of origin.

Main religious festivals

Christmas – birth of Jesus.
Good Friday and **Easter Sunday** usually in March or April.
Good Friday commemorates the crucifixion of Jesus.
Easter Sunday commemorates the resurrection of Jesus from the dead.

Holy day

Sunday

What followers believe

Christians believe in the One God, but this unity contains three Persons – the Trinity: the Father – God, the Son – Jesus and the Holy Spirit – the belief that the spirit within the individual is guiding us and is also creating a community such as the church.

Most Christians believe that Jesus is the Son of God and that God revealed Himself in Jesus. In him, the One God, Creator of heaven and earth, came down to earth in human form. This is the doctrine of incarnation – God became human through Jesus and so possesses both human and divine natures. Jesus took upon himself the sins that separate humanity from God and reconciled human beings with God and God with human beings. This is called atonement (making 'one' again) and

Christians believe that atonement is achieved through the sacrificial death of Jesus. Where once human beings had offered sacrifices to God as a sin offering, now Jesus offered Himself as the one sacrifice for all human sin. Jesus died and came back to life and this is called the resurrection. Later he was taken up into heaven in what is called the ascension.

Christians believe that those who believe in the incarnation, atonement and resurrection of Jesus will have all their sins forgiven and will be raised to new life when Jesus returns to this world in the Second Coming.

> *I like being a Christian . . . I always feel I've got a friend because Jesus is always there. I like being part of a big community where you're always welcome . . . I believe that I'm going to spend eternity in Heaven with my Almighty Father and I need to tell anyone and everyone about God's amazing promise. I believe God loves everyone equally and immensely and there is nothing that he wouldn't do to be with us.*

Josh

 Islam

How and by whom founded

Muhammad ibn Abdullah – Muhammad son of Abdullah, born in Mecca in Saudi Arabia in the sixth century received his first divine revelation from Allah through the angel Jibril – Gabriel whilst meditating in a cave near Mecca. Around 610 CE Muhammad began preaching that he was the messenger of the One True God Allah – the same God who is worshipped in the Jewish and Christian faiths. The words revealed to him were memorised and later written down by his followers in a book called the Qur'an – literally means 'recite'. Such is the reverence for Muhammad that whenever Muslims speak his name they respectfully say after it, 'peace be upon him'.

After the death of Muhammad in 632 CE, the Muslim community split. Those who chose Abu Bakr as Muhammad's successor became the Sunni Muslims, the followers of the Sunna – traditions of the Prophet Muhammad. Those who chose Muhammad's nearest relative, his cousin and son-in-law Ali, to succeed him became the Shi'at 'Ali – party of Ali, the Shi'a Muslims. Not much separates the two groups in belief and practice, but Shi'as place more emphasis on their Imams, a succession of leaders, who are regarded as a line of inspired teachers.

Sunni Muslims account for some 90 per cent of the world's Islamic population. One main centre of Sunni Islam is Saudi Arabia, which is also the place where Islam's holiest site is found – the Ka'ba at Mecca. Shi'a Muslims, many of whom live in Iran and Iraq, account for the remaining 10 per cent.

Language

Arabic, Farsi (Persian), Urdu, Punjabi, or the language of the country of origin.

Main religious festivals

Eid-al-Fitr when people say special prayers of thanks, give each other gifts and wear new clothes. Festival takes place after *Ramadan*, the month of fasting.
Eid-al-Adha is the festival of sacrifice recalling the sacrificial ram God gave to Abraham in place of his son; coincides with the end of *Hajj* – month of pilgrimage to Mecca.

Holy day

Friday

What followers believe

Islam is a whole way of life with guidelines for the moral, legal, spiritual and political organisation of society. Muslims believe that the prophet Muhammad is the last of the many prophets of God mentioned in the Old and New Testament. Islam is based on five major beliefs know as the arkan ad-din – Five Pillars. The Five Pillars begin with an affirmation of faith – that is to declare belief that Allah is the only God and that Muhammad is his prophet. Then to pray daily five times, give money to the poor, fast during the ninth month of the Islamic calendar called Ramadan in the daylight hours and make a hajj – pilgrimage to Mecca at least once in a lifetime for those who are able.

Both men and women are required to dress modestly. Muslims cover their heads and bodies in accordance with the words of Allah in the Qur'an, 24: 31. As Islam is a world faith, people in different countries wear different clothes in interpretation of the Qur'an.

> *I enjoy my faith, I enjoy my belief . . . when people see me covered in hijab they think, oh poor me or my husband must have done that to me but I think they've got it so wrong . . . it isn't a burden . . . I choose to cover . . . It doesn't change the person I am because I'm outwardly manifesting my faith by wearing my scarf. My religion is a structure that holds my life together. So many people make the religion harder than it needs to be . . . we enjoy ourselves as female Muslims . . . the social aspect of faith is very important. My belief is an inherent part of me but I do it through love and understanding not because it is forced upon me in any way.*
>
> Anisa

Stop and Think: you/colleagues

- How do you relate to those of other beliefs and none?
- What ways do your religious beliefs or lack of religious beliefs influence the way you work with others?
- Discuss ways to work with young people to encourage understanding and respect for people with religious beliefs that they do not share.
- Talk about the differences between religious, cultural and national identity.

Stop and Think: you/colleagues/young people

- How do you relate to people with other beliefs?
- How do you relate to people with no beliefs?
- How do you relate to people who have the same beliefs as you?
- If you could create your own religion, what beliefs would be important?

Here are two activities that aim to encourage thought about personal belief:

Group Activity: you/colleagues/young people

What do You Believe?

Purpose: To think about personal beliefs.
Preparation: Make sets of 14 cards with one statement on each card.
Method: Before starting the activity establish and agree the group boundaries (see Preface).

In small groups, one person turns over the cards and reads the statement. Each member of the group agrees or disagrees with the statement and says why. In large group, pool ideas.

- Animals have feelings.
- God is an old man with a white beard.
- So called psychics are all con artists.
- Religions are the major cause of most of the wars in the world.
- Being spiritual is not about going to a place of worship.
- People should have the freedom to worship as they please.
- Horoscopes are scary.
- I often have 'déjà vu' – the feeling of having already experienced a present situation.
- There is no life after death.
- The good guys always lose.
- Football is my religion.
- Man does not live by bread alone.
- War is always wrong.
- Humans invented gods to provide answers for things they could not explain.

Group Activity: you/colleagues/young people

The Belief Game

Purpose: To think about personal beliefs.
Preparation: Make sets of 20 cards with one belief on each card.
Method: Before starting the activity establish and agree the group boundaries (see Preface).

Everyone receives a set of 20 'belief' cards. Working on your own, sit on the floor and set cards out with the card closest to you that most represents your beliefs and the card furthest from you that most represents what you least believe. Think about the belief that means most and means least. Pick out some of the beliefs that are common to the group and discuss. Examples of beliefs to write on cards:

- Belief in ghosts.
- Belief that people are basically good.

- Belief that people are basically bad.
- Belief in the same things as family.
- Belief that one particular political party is the best political party.
- Belief in atheism – the absence of belief in God.
- Belief that cloning animals helps save lives.
- Belief in making the world a better place.
- Belief in the greatest happiness for the greatest number of people.
- Belief in ridding the world of poverty.
- Belief in a particular religion.
- Belief in God.
- Belief in the same way as when little.
- Belief that God made the world.
- Belief that God is all-powerful, all-knowing and all-loving.
- Belief that the body has a soul.
- Belief that religion makes you a better person.
- Belief that cruelty to animals is the worst type of cruelty.
- Belief in UFOs.
- Belief in horoscopes.

Chapter 8

What About Spirituality?

This chapter examines the concept of spirituality. It looks at how we can relate to the spiritual dimension in our own lives and discusses the introduction of spiritual development into work with young people. Throughout the chapter there are questionnaires for you to do alone. There are 'Stop and Think' points that can be used in discussion with colleagues and young people. At the end of the chapter activities are suggested for colleagues and young people.

Spiritual belief cannot be packaged as easily as a belief in a particular religion or philosophy. Perhaps, it is easier to start by saying what spiritual belief is not. It is not necessarily a belief in spirits or ghosts. It is not necessarily a belief in one faith. And now can we say what a spiritual belief is? Well, perhaps it is an inner reality, an intuitive belief that there is something essential, something more and 'other' than the material world. Spirituality is about being aware of our own insignificance in the large scheme of things. Spirituality is beyond and at the same time part of organised religion, specific culture, individual background and everyday life.

In many ways, spirituality is what we have most in common with other people. However different are our ways of life, the issues that are most important remain the same for everyone. issues like why are we here and where are we going. Many issues that involve our inner thoughts and feelings and many issues that involve the wider world. There is a large element of doubt and uncertainty when we think about these issues. And maybe that is a good thing because undoubtedly, uncertainty about great problems stimulates human beings to think more deeply. It's like scientific investigation. Good science provides evidence about the natural world, but is seldom certain. We cannot explain the many mysteries of life. It turns out that we can visualise only about four per cent of the universe – the rest is made up of so-called dark matter, which is still completely incomprehensible. So perhaps, spirituality is an open-minded, questioning belief that accepts that there is more to life than what we see.

> *For me, spirituality isn't about God . . . it's about my own personal rules that guide my behaviour, about my sense of self and belonging, about what it is to exist and be a part of the world, about lots of things I don't understand but hope to learn more about.*
>
> Dixon

Stop and Think: you/colleagues

- What is spirituality?
- What is spiritual development?
- How to recognise our own spiritual self: what is it that makes spirituality part of our being?
- How does our own spiritual development influence the way in which we work with young people?
- What activities could help young people to notice aspects that they find spiritual in the world around them?

- In the Western world there is a growing polarisation between those who live by religious beliefs and those who do not. How can spiritual development help to bridge the gap?

Spirituality within personal awareness and development

Spiritual development starts with a closer understanding of our own and other people's personal and social values and a broader vision of our place in the world. Personal awareness and development is a way into spiritual development that may or may not take place within a faith tradition.

Personal awareness is about getting to know ourselves. If we know ourselves a little more, it is easier to get to know others a little more. If we try to understand why we believe what we believe and how that affects the way we live our lives, we are more likely to try and understand what and why other people believe and how it affects the way they live their lives.

This may lead us to a change of attitude, a greater self-esteem and a greater confidence in our relationships with others. The basic tool we need is an open mind that is prepared to ask the kind of questions that we asked without any thought when very young like 'who am I?' and 'what am I for?' Questions that often disappear when we reach adolescence.

Digging deep into ourselves and asking searching questions that help us to know ourselves isn't a new idea. In ancient Greece, the philosopher Plotinus considered introspection and fine-tuning essential for personal development:

> *Withdraw into yourself and if you do not like what you see, act as a sculptor. Cut away here, smooth there, make this line lighter, that one purer. Never cease carving until there shines out from you the Godlike sphere of character.*

Schulweis, 1995: 42

Stop and Think: you/colleagues

Here is a questionnaire for you to complete either on your own or with your colleagues. There are no right or wrong answers and some of the questions may lead to other questions that you may or may not have answers for at the moment. If using this questionnaire with a group of colleagues, individual feed-back can be followed by a general discussion:

- What does 'personal awareness' mean to me?
- What does 'personal development' mean to me?
- What experience have I had of personal development?
- What areas of myself have I developed?
- What areas would I like to develop?
- What does 'spiritual awareness' mean to me?
- How does personal awareness link with spiritual awareness?
- What direct experience have I had of spiritual awareness?
- What does 'spiritual development' mean to me?
- How does personal development link with spiritual development?
- Do I associate spiritual awareness with religion? If so, why?
- What are my spiritual needs?

- Do I know anyone who I think of as having spiritual qualities?
- If so, what are they?

Morality – understanding good and bad behaviour – is a key component of personal awareness and development and as such is an integral part in our search for spirituality. As we begin to get to know ourselves and look at what our lives are really about, we inevitably start to think about the way we treat other people and the way we treat the earth.

How we learn personal morality is a fairly easy question: ingrained opinions learnt from family, formal religion, culture and friends. How we develop our own morality is a more challenging question. Experience, intuition, an examination of personal thoughts, words and actions alongside an investigation into our inherited value system are perhaps part of the answer.

Spirituality Chart

Personal	One's own; individual; private
Awareness	Being conscious; knowing
Development	Changing over time in response to understanding and circumstances
Religion	Overall and external structure; system of faith and worship
Morality	A knowledge of what is right and what is wrong. A judgment taken on a moral decision or action that is considered to be the 'correct' thing to think or do. For example, you may think that not harming oneself and others and the environment is a moral thing to do.
Ethics	Code of conduct concerning questions of ethical importance; moral principles
Belief	In a non-religious sense, the term 'belief' is used when something is true because it is proven. For example, it is a fact that a triangle has three sides. In a religious sense, 'belief' is a strong conviction that cannot be proved.
Faith	In a non-religious sense, the term 'faith'is a synonym for 'trust', 'reliance' or 'confidence'. For example, you may say that you trust a friend to help you when necessary. Religious people refer to belief in such terms.
Spirituality	Innate/search for purpose/action in the world/awe-inspiring experience

Stop and Think: you/colleagues/young people

Consider a major moral issue where people hold opposing views. For example: cloning embryos, abortion and euthanasia. What is your view and what is the opposing point of view? Try and find three arguments that challenge your own view.

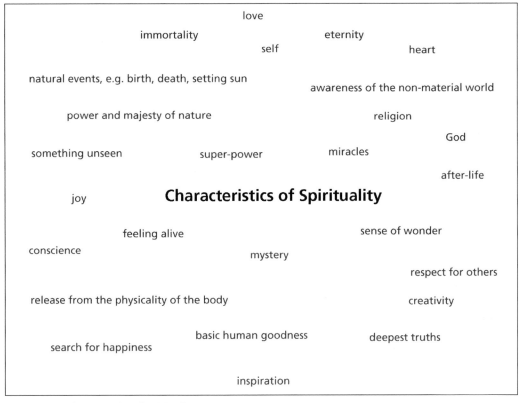

Diagram 1 – Characteristics of Spirituality

Spirituality within faith traditions

Organised religion is an external structure that systemises faith and worship. Within each religion there is diversity of practice and belief. Religion offers a framework for questions that people have always asked such as 'how did life start', 'why was I born', 'what happens to me when I die'. Religion suggests answers to these important questions that are part of spiritual development.

Like all ideas, institutions and organisations, individuals can use religion as a force for good or bad: religion can abuse and can be abused. Religion is abused when it is perceived as the cause of all hatred and its genuine spiritual values are discarded. Many of the world's finest principles have their origins in organised religion.

Buddhism

Just as a mother would protect her only child with her life, even so let one cultivate a boundless love towards all beings.

Khuddaka Patha, from the Metta Sutta

 Christianity

Do to others as you would have them do to you.

Luke 6: 31

 Hinduism

This is the sum of duty: do naught to others which if done to thee would cause thee pain.

Mahabharata 5:1517

 Islam

No one of you is a believer until he desires for his brother that which he desires for himself.

An-Nawani's Forty Hadith, 13

 Judaism

What is hateful to you, do not do to your fellow man.

Talmud: Shabbat 31a

 Sikhism

No one is my enemy, and no one is a stranger. I get along with everyone.

The Guru Granth Sahib 1299

In many cultures, religion has played a crucial role in addressing the spiritual nature of the human being as well as in promoting social order. And religion continues to provide the shared beliefs and moral vision that unite many people into communities. One such community is at Tashi Jong, Himachal Pradesh in the foothills of the Himilayas in Northern India. Here young Tibetan Buddhist women have made difficult and dangerous journeys over the Himalayan Mountains in order to retrieve their heritage that was destroyed during the communist takeover in Tibet. They are now studying Buddhist philosophy and practice and the Tibetan and English language. They also make handicrafts and some are learning traditional painting and tailoring (www.tenzinpalmo.com/DGL).

I'm happy now because I feel like by being here I am able to accomplish more, to develop my mind more, to be able to understand other people more, to be able to help more here at Tashi Jong.

Tenzin Chozom

Just as religion can be abused, religion can abuse when it perpetrates sexism, self-righteousness and hatred of the 'other'. When it degrades and dehumanises members of another faith or denies them their basic equality, rights and dignity. There are some people in every denomination of every religion who use the symbols and texts of religion for their own selfish purposes. Northern Ireland with its longstanding traditional religious divide between Catholics and Protestants is an example. Extremists on both sides of the divide have used religion to validate unjust behaviour towards the other. The same can be said with regard to the London bombings in July 2005, the continuing troubles in Iraq and between India and Pakistan.

As far as organised religion is concerned, the assumption underlying this book is that although there are overlaps, there are also distinctions between spirituality and organised religion. Many people are looking for spirituality without necessarily looking at organised religion. As a practical example, it is noticeable that in many bookshops, larger and larger selections of books on 'Soul, Mind and Body' are appearing. These books are often located next to an even larger selection of books on personal development/self-help and near to a much smaller selection on religion. Have we reached a point in Western society where religion is no longer necessary in order to bring spirituality into our lives? Or maybe, the spiritual element within religion as practised in the West needs re-emphasising? Perhaps there is a case for less doctrine and dogma and more wonder and wisdom.

Spirituality with or without a faith tradition

The three diagrams include many words that are associated with the concept of spirituality. They focus on the characteristics of spirituality, spiritual needs and the tools that can help in exploring spiritual awareness and development. Before the first two there is a Stop and Think point.

Stop and Think: you/colleagues

- From Diagram 1, pick three characteristics of spirituality that are relevant to you.
- Think about why you have chosen these particular characteristics and what they mean to you.

Stop and Think: you/colleagues

The needs in Diagram 2 are called 'spiritual' because they help us to establish a sense of self and to fulfil a meaningful life. Choose three and explain why they are relevant to you and how they affect the way you behave towards other people.

Diagram 2 – Spiritual Needs

Stop and Think: you/colleagues

- From Diagram 3 (following) make a list and choose the tools that you already use.
- Now make a list from the same diagram of which tools you can use with young people.
- Think about this and discuss within group.

There are many definitions for the concept of spirituality. Here are four to think about:

1. Spirituality is innate.
2. Spirituality is a search for purpose.
3. Spirituality is action in the world.
4. Spirituality is an awe-inspiring experience.

1. Spirituality is inate

This definition suggests that we are born with a spiritual dimension. We can see this in the very young. The kind of delight a young child displays when looking at the leaves of a tree for the first time. And the kind of thirst for knowledge the child demonstrates when incessantly asking 'why this, why that, why, why, why?'

Hay and Nye in their book, *The Spirit of the Child* present the biologist Alister Hardy's view that in the same way that breathing and eating are natural phenomena, so too is spiritual awareness. Hardy considers that spiritual awareness has helped the individual to survive and therefore has remained part of the human make-up:

> *There is a form of awareness, different from and transcending everyday awareness, which is potentially present in all human beings and which has a positive function in enabling individuals to survive in their natural environment.*

Hay and Nye, 1998: 10

Innate spirituality is a heightened awareness of what's going on both outside and inside us. But this acute awareness disappears as we grow up. Questions such as 'where have I come from, where am I going, what am I meant to do' are not usually asked by about the age of 12. Often at the same stage that children in the western world first encounter rational scientific ideas, spiritual scepticism steps in (49–50).

But even if Hay and Nye are correct in their analysis that natural spirituality declines as we grow older; it does not necessarily have to disappear forever. Personal development can lead to an awareness of latent innate spirituality. To an awareness that deep within us there is something unique that connects us with all humanity and by which we recognise that we, as individuals, are more than mere flesh and bone.

In the same way as questions lead to knowledge for the young child, questions are an integral part of our adult search for knowledge of our essential purpose in life.

2. Spirituality is a search for purpose

We cannot search for the essential purpose of our lives without a growing understanding of our selves. So in a sense, knowing the 'self' is a stage on the way to spirituality. The self can be defined

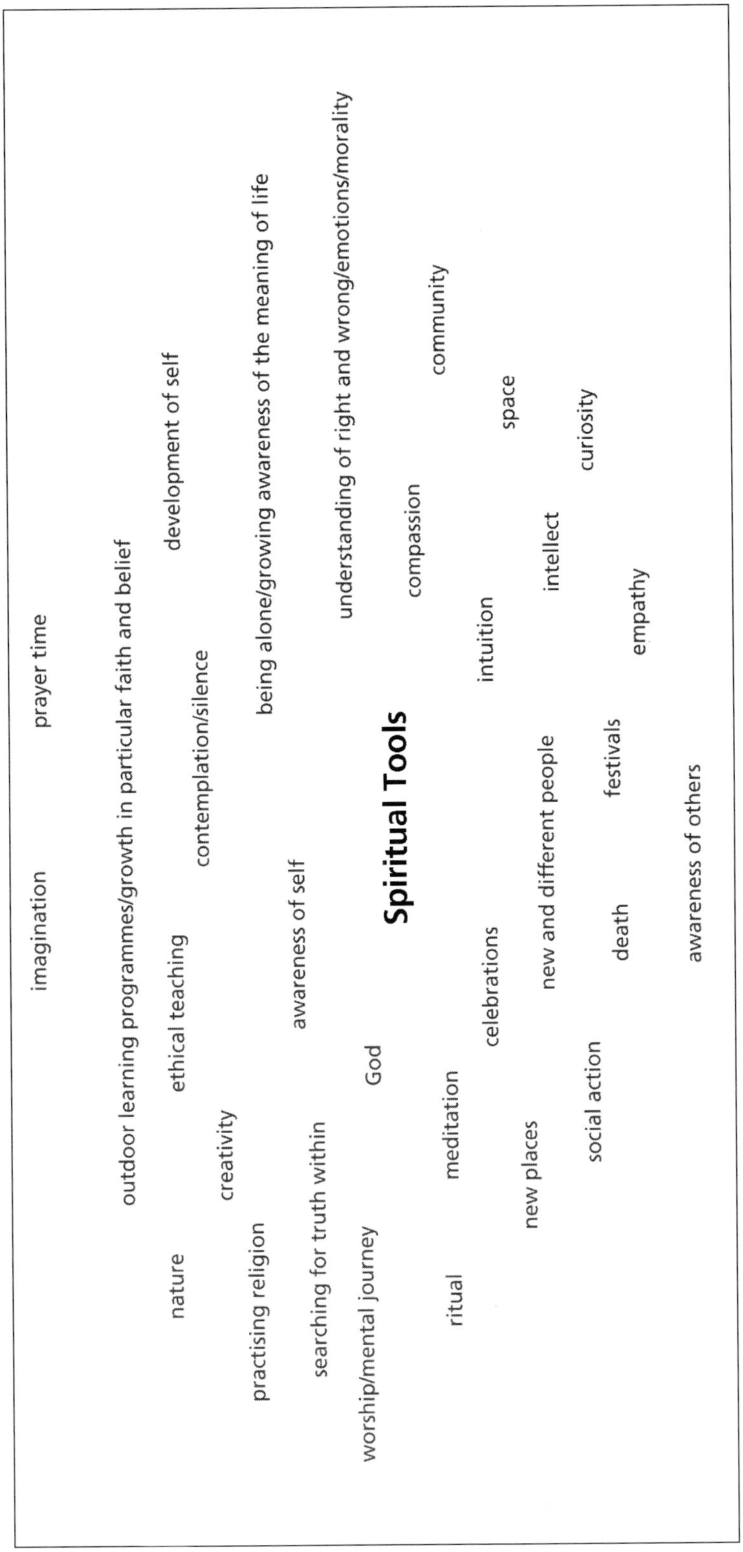

nature

practising religion

searching for truth within

worship/mental journey

God

ritual

meditation

new places

social action

imagination

outdoor learning programmes/growth in particular faith and belief

ethical teaching

creativity

awareness of self

celebrations

new and different people

death

festivals

awareness of others

prayer time

contemplation/silence

development of self

being alone/growing awareness of the meaning of life

understanding of right and wrong/emotions/morality

community

space

curiosity

compassion

intuition

intellect

empathy

Spiritual Tools

Diagram 3 – Spiritual Tools

as the absolute unique essence contained in each human being. Perhaps, this unique essence is the innate component in every baby born that is described in the first definition of spirituality:

> *Some call the self 'conscience' and some call it 'soul'. To me, on my 'believing in God' days, it is the divine spark . . . that tiny bit of God that is in everyone. It is in everyone because everyone is made in the image of God.*

Linda

We all have the potential to make sense of our lives. And it is often when deep emotions are felt at traumatic times like those of death and illness, birth and falling in love that we start to ask questions like 'what's it all about?' and 'what's the point?' Sometimes, these questions are painful to think or talk about.

Although talking about spirituality does not happen very often, research suggests that it is thought about and experienced. In 1965, Alister Hardy founded the Religious Experience Research Unit in Oxford. Much of its research has shown that a surprisingly wide range of people do have spiritual experiences, including those who would not describe themselves as religious people. A detailed study of the spiritual experiences of young people revealed that nearly 80 per cent of a sample of 6,500 admitted to having had some kind of experience that could be described as spiritual. 'Spiritual' was described as an experience of being 'at peace with a strong desire to find meaning and purpose in life . . . a feeling of being part of a mysterious whole' (Hay and Nye, 44).

3. Spirituality is action in the world

Spirituality is about engaging in the world in every sense. In the experience of nature and creativity, in our relationships and in every intention and action that leads to a more meaningful experience and positive result. So we can say that human rights, ecology and ethical globalisation are all universal spiritual issues.

Engaging in the world often happens through community. Father Bruno Hussar, a Catholic priest, founded a village in Israel where both Jewish and Arab people live. He wrote that:

> *Although most of the peace workers in the village are not religious in the conventional sense they are deeply spiritual beings on account of the spiritual work they undertake.*

Feuerverger, 124

These peace workers are part of a secular community. Some of them are professional facilitators who lead residential encounter workshops for young Arabs and Jews. They are engaged in the spiritual action of getting young Arabs and Jews to talk to each other. The work they undertake demonstrates care for other people – one of the basic tenets of all of the world's faiths. And yet mostly they are not religious. Spiritual work is indeed found within and without religious traditions.

> *A sense of community is important to me. I think that's what I find most helpful in spiritual traditions. I haven't had a religious background but I've had exposure to religious traditions and that sense of tradition of thinking about the big questions in life that you find in communities. I define spirituality as trying to work out what our higher relevance is both individually and at a community level.*

Daniel

4. Spirituality is an awe-inspiring experience

'Awe' isn't 'fear' in the conventional sense. It is more a feeling of deep wonder: wonder of the natural world, God and the supernatural and a realisation of how insignificant human beings are in the larger scheme of things.

> *There are so many connotations around spirituality – forget the word faith, maybe it is just complete honesty with the fact of our complete frightening smallness and helplessness – a kind of surrender.*
>
> Tenzin Chozom

The German theologian, Rudolf Otto in his book *The Idea of the Holy* coined the term 'numinous' to describe the irrational *mysterium tremendum,* an awe-filled mystery that leaves us trembling (Scholem, 1995: 57). That kind of experience does happen sometimes. Listen to an astronomer speaking about the planets, observe the birth of a baby or view the sun rising over the sea at dawn and you will know instinctively what this means:

> *I get a deep spiritual uplift when I go surfing . . . the power and majesty of the ocean really gets through to me. I'm released from the physicality of the body and in that experience I understand spirituality . . . to me it is the interconnectedness between the physical and the non-physical.*
>
> Joe

Spiritual development when working with young people

This chapter shows how intangible spirituality is and how many ways there are of describing and of expressing our spirituality. As far as young people are concerned, we are facilitators enabling them to find their own spirituality in their own time. They need the space to explore life in all its complexity. This means the opportunity to discover new ideas, skills, activities and experiences. They need the chance to develop a deeper understanding of themselves. This means listening and responding in a sensitive way.

Spiritual development is a two-way process. We are, in the act of helping others to develop, developing ourselves. We are giving our everyday work an added dimension. This is risky, this is challenging. But that is so much of what spirituality is about.

Stop and Think: you/colleagues

- The difference between a material and a spiritual world-view.
- The difference between spirituality, morality, religion and faith.
- What are spiritual issues: human rights – freedom of religion, politics and speech, ethical globalisation, cloning, etc.
- What are spiritual practices: yoga, meditation, creativity, serving the community, worship, etc.
- What activities could encourage young people to think about their own spirituality.
- In the group, have you come to a definition of spirituality? what it isn't? and what it is?

Group activities: young people

Outdoor activities

Outdoor activities are one way youth work can be used to develop the spirit as well as the body. They can provide opportunities for developmental and value-forming experiences. It is remarkable the questions and discussions that can be started by young people just lying on the ground looking at the stars or sitting on a mountain. Or the conversation that can be gently directed as for example after the activity of rock climbing. Rock climbing is an activity where young people have to learn to trust other people. Talked about later in a group, this experience is useful for young people to question situations where trust is involved both ways – who do they trust? and who trusts them? (Robertson, 2005: 65).

Several books on outdoor activities are recommended in the bibliography.

Activity: young people

The Spiritual and Non-Spiritual World View

Aim: To introduce the idea of spirituality and to consider the difference between the spiritual (non-material and non-physical) and non-spiritual (material and physical) world-view.

Preparation: Prepare 20 laminated cards. On ten cards write a word associated with the spiritual world-view. On the other ten cards write a word associated with the non-spiritual world-view.

Method: Hold up each card and ask members of the group to place it on one of the three piles:

- Words associated with the non-spiritual world-view for example car, clothes, make-up, I-pods, money, holidays, travel, fair.

- Words associated with the spiritual world-view for example love, dreams, life after life, friends, people, heaven.

- Words associated with a mixture of both the spiritual and the non-spiritual world-view for example holidays, relationships, money, books, computers.

Discuss: Why is one word associated with spirituality and another word not?
What makes it spiritual?
What makes it not spiritual?
How would you describe your own world-view?
How would you describe spirituality?
How easy or difficult is it to distinguish between a spiritual and non-spiritual world-view?
What is the difference?

The 20 'Commandments'
(The top 20 contemporary values chosen by 4,000 people in a YouGov poll, 2005)

Purpose: To develop own spiritual framework.

Preparation: Prepare sets of cards with a written 'commandment' on each card

Method: Everyone receives a set of 'commandments'. Place 'commandments' in numerical order of how important they are to you. Number one is the most important and number 20 is the least important.

Talk about how and why you chose the 'commandments'. Discuss what the 'commandments' mean and how they contribute to society. Develop the idea by creating your own 'commandments'.

- Be honest
- Be true to your own God
- Don't kill
- Be true to yourself
- Look after the vulnerable
- Protect your family
- Respect your mother and father
- Try your best at all times
- Enjoy life
- Look after your health
- Nothing in excess
- Don't commit adultery
- Live within your means
- Appreciate what you have
- Never be violent
- Protect the environment
- Protect and nurture children
- Don't steal
- Take responsibility for your own actions
- Treat others, as you would have them treat you

Conclusion

In the course of writing this book, I have spoken to people from different faith and non-faith traditions. The conversations made me realise how much we have in common once we rid ourselves of the many preconceptions that come from sheer ignorance and feelings of superiority.

The way to a more peaceful world depends upon the way we treat people. The moral philosopher Mary Warnock remarked that we treat people that we know better than people that we do not know. So it seems to me, that we as professionals, who work with young people, have an urgent need to get to know and understand more people.

Getting to know others involves knowing ourselves and thus much of this book is about personal development. We need to know what we think about our own traditions or lack of them so that we can openly express and exchange views with people from different backgrounds to ourselves. By such talk, we are sewing the seeds for a more integrated society that has no space for entrenched extremist views to grow. By such talk, we can begin to create a world-view that transcends all cultures and creeds. A spiritual world-view that helps us and helps the young people we work with to relate to the world in a responsible way.

Writing this book has enabled me to think about the differences between personal and spiritual development, religion and faith, and has allowed me to address the questions racing through my mind. I do so hope some of these questions are your questions. Now, I have come to the end of the beginning of the journey – a journey that values and celebrates diversity and yet at the same time is rooted in a strong sense of self-identity. I hope you will continue your journey with me.

Glossary

Adler, Alfred (1870–1937) – Austrian psychiatrist; introduced the term inferiority feeling, later widely called inferiority complex.

Allah – The name used for God by Muslims – adherents of Islam.

Agnosticism – The belief that we do not know whether God exists or not.

Anthropocentric – (*Anthro* – man in Greek) centring on human beings.

Anthropomorphism – Attribute human form or personality to God.

Archetype – The word 'archetype' comes from the Greek *arche* meaning first and from the Greek *type* meaning imprint or pattern.

Aristotle (384–322 BCE) – Greek philosopher whose work includes dialogues, constitutions, histories, literary criticism, poetry, essays, philosophies and scientific compilations.

Aryan – Word describing the Caucasian people who invaded India around 2000 BCE and who gradually imposed their language and culture upon the earlier inhabitants. Related peoples settled in Iran and Mesopotamia.

Ascension – A Christian term describing Jesus' departure back to heaven, there to stay until his return to earth at the time of the second resurrection.

Atheism – The belief that gods or God does not exist.

Atonement – Literally 'at-one-ment'; need for atonement is felt by many people with and without faith. Christians believe that atonement is achieved through the sacrificial death of Jesus. See also Yom Kippur the Jewish Day of Atonement.

BCE – Before Common Era, i.e. before the time of Jesus.

Bhagavad-Gita (The Song of the Lord) – part of the Hindu sacred writings; the central section of the *Mahabharata* written in the third or second century BCE. A conversation between Arjuna and Krishna that explores the essential questions of life.

Bible – Scriptures of the Old and New Testament.

Brahman – The origin and cause of all existence, according to Hinduism.

Buddha – Siddhartha Gautama (448–368 BCE), the founder of Buddhism born in Lumbini in the foothills of the Himalayas in North India.

Buddhism – In some of its many different forms, Buddhism is the religion without a god. Buddhism began historically when the Buddha (see above) attained 'enlightenment', the ultimate truth by which people are freed from the cycle of rebirth.

Brunner, Emile (1889–1966) – Swiss Christian theologian in the Reformed tradition who helped direct the course of modern Protestant theology.

Christianity – Founded on the worship of Jesus, a teacher and healer who was born a Jew in Bethlehem over 2000 years ago.

CE – Common Era, i.e. after Jesus was born.

Darwin, Charles Robert (1809–1882) – English naturalist who developed a biological theory of natural selection that influenced the course of philosophic thought. Most famous book: *The Origin of the Species by Means of Natural Selection* (1859).

Day of Judgement – Belief traditionally held by Jews, Christians and Muslims that the soul lives on at death and on the Day of Judgement it may be reunited with its body or exist in some new spiritual form.

Deism – Belief in the existence of a god without accepting that the One God was revealed to human-beings through an agent; characteristic of natural religion.

Determinism – Philosophical theory that human action is not free but determined by motives regarded as external forces acting on the will.

Dharma – In Hinduism, the eternal law of the universe. In Buddhism, the teachings of the Buddha.

Eastern Salvationist Tradition – Also known as the Mystical Tradition, it stresses that God is found within the human spirit and that life on earth involves a spiritual journey in order to achieve a direct experience of God.

Enlightenment – According to Buddhism, understanding the truth about the way things are.

Epicurus (341–270 BCE) – Greek philosopher influenced by Plato, mainly interested in Ethics. He taught that the highest good for humans to aim at is peacefulness of mind, body and spirit.

European Renaissance – Literally a 'rebirth' of the art and culture of antiquity. The Renaissance began in the late 14th century in Northern Italy and spread rapidly northward during the 15th and 16th centuries.

Eysenck, Hans Jurgen (1916–94) – German-born British psychologist who developed a system to ascertain personality type.

Fatalism – Belief that all events are determined to happen the way they do whatever we do to try to avoid or prevent them – 'what will be will be'.

Five Pillars of Islam – The five principal duties for Muslims: the profession of faith in the One God, daily prayer, charitable giving, fasting during the month of Ramadan, pilgrimage to Mecca.

French Enlightenment – 18th century movement also known as the Age of Reason. Philosophers including Voltaire and Rousseau advocated questioning inherited truths, rationalism, education for everybody and natural religion, i.e. getting rid of irrational dogma that is attached to religious teaching.

Freud, Sigmund (1856 1939) – Viennese neurologist who focused on the role of the unconscious processes as motivators of behaviour as well as many other concepts and principles governing the human mind.

Gandhi, Mahatma (1869–1948) – Lawyer who struggled for Indian independence from Britain, Hindu-Muslim unity, the eradication of the caste system and the emancipation of women.

Gibran, Kahil (1883–1931) – Lebanese-American philosopher and poet.

Gospels – From old English 'godspel' meaning 'good news' (as the Greek 'evangelion'). The four accounts in Christianity's New Testament of Jesus' life and ministry.

Guru – A spiritual leader and a teacher in many religions including Hinduism and Sikhism. Also in Sikhism the title for one of the ten early leaders of the faith.

Guru Granth Sahib – The Sikhs holiest scriptures, also known as Adi Granth (first book), treated as if it were a revered teacher.

Guru Nanak – First leader of the Sikh religion (1469 – 1538 CE), born in Talwandi, near Lahore.

Haddith – In Islam, the collection of sayings and traditions of the Prophet Muhammad.

Hebrew Bible – The Pentateuch, i.e. the first five books of the Bible plus the writings of the prophets. In non-Jewish circles known as the Old Testament.

Hick, John – Born 1922, British theologian and philosopher of religion.

Hinduism – The word 'Hindu' is derived from the Persian word for Indian, and Hinduism is traditionally the religion of the peoples of India: a cluster of religious beliefs and practices that have grown up over the past 4.500 years in the Indian subcontinent.

Hubris – Recognised in classical Greek ethical and religious thought as overweening pride leading to an insult to the gods.

Humanism – A philosophical belief focusing on people and not on gods or the One God.

Immanence – God within the individual person as well as permanently pervading the material world.

Incarnation – Literally 'enfleshment', the Christian belief that in the historical life of Jesus, God became man without ceasing to be God.

Islam – Derived from the Arabic word for 'submission' or 'obedience', it is the religion practised by Muslims. It is based on the teaching of Muhammad ibn Abdullah Allah, known as the Prophet Muhammad, who is believed to have received the revealed word of Allah (God) some 1,400 years ago, in what is now Saudi Arabia.

Judaism – The first of the world's faiths to accept as its central belief that there is only one God. No single founder but Abraham, Isaac and Jacob together with Sarah, Rachel and Leah are revered as the ancestors of the Jewish people.

Jung, Carl Gustav (1875–1961) – Swiss psychologist, a student and follower of Freud. Known for his word association techniques and his ideas on the Personal and Collective Unconscious.

Karma – Sanskrit word for 'work' or 'action'. In Hinduism and Buddhism, the eternal law of cause and effect. Thus the law of karma maintains that you get a position in life according to how good or bad you were in the previous life. Your present condition, your happiness and status are directly the result of your previous life. Consequently, you are wholly responsible for your life now and in the future.

Khalsa – The community of pure, fully initiated Sikhs.

Laws of Manu – Part of the *Smriti* (memory) Hindu sacred writings. The Laws of Manu ('man', a kind of Adam) has 12 books with 2685 verses, and was written in 200–100 BCE. The books give detailed instructions on what people may or may not do, marriage laws, diet rules, daily and death rites, etc.

Liturgy – Form of public worship set down in book.

Maimonides, Moses – 12th century medical doctor, philosopher of Judaism and codifier of Biblical and Talmudic laws.

Mandela, Nelson (1918–present) – Political activist who struggled to bring an end to institutionalised racial discrimination in South Africa.

Materialism – The idea that the physical world is all there is.

Maya Religion – Between 100 BCE and 250 CE the Maya people developed the cult of the rulers, built pyramids and religious objects. Main centres were the Yucatan peninsular, Guatemala, Belize, parts of Honduras, El Salvador and the Mexican state. Religion survived until the arrival and conquest by the Spaniards in 1524.

Messiah – Hebrew word for 'anointed'; in Judaism the deliverer of the Jewish people as foretold in the Hebrew Bible. In the Christian tradition, Jesus Christ, whom Christians believe to be the Saviour of humankind.

Moksha – In the Hindu tradition, a Sanskrit word meaning release from the ongoing cycle of birth, death and rebirth. Moksha is achieved when virtue, knowledge and love of God cancel out the weight of Karma that requires the self to be reborn.

Monotheism – Doctrine that there is only one God.

Moral Law – Rules for living that are concerned with the distinction between right and wrong.

Muhammad Ibn 'Abn Allah – Lived 570–632, founder and prophet of Islam.

Myth – A sacred story that originates and circulates within a particular community. Some myths explain puzzling physical phenomena or customs, institutions and practices whose origin in the community would otherwise be mysterious.

Mysticism – A system of contemplative prayer and spirituality aimed at achieving direct intuitive experience of the supernatural or the divine; it is a view held in many religions.

New Testament – The collection of gospels, epistles and related works that were accepted amongst Christians as Holy Scripture by about 300 CE.

Pali – Ma'agadhi was the original name for Pali and was the language current in the land of Magadha (parts of North India and Pakistan) during the time of the Buddha. Now Pali is the name for an important Buddhist text.

Piaget, Jean (1896–1980) – Swiss psychologist who was enormously influential in establishing developmental psychology and showing how cognition and intelligence develop during the years of childhood.

Plato (428–348 BCE) – Greek philosopher who based many of his writings on Socrates' life and thought. Famous for his Dialogues which include discussions on the immortality of the soul.

Plotinus (CE 205–270) – Greek philosopher influenced by Plato and famous for the Enneads (Six Sets) written down after his death by his student Porphyry.

Predestination – Theological theory that all events that have happened, are happening and will happen have been predetermined to happen and are being caused to happen by God.

Predeterminism – Philosophical theory that every event has a cause that is activated at an exact time and at no other time, in accordance with the will of some operating principle. Maybe God, natural necessity or the ancient idea of eternal forms.

Primal Religions – Religions that are *prior* to those often known as the *universal* religions. Primal religions are the religions of small-scale pre-literate societies. They have no religious writings or scriptures. Instead, beliefs are handed down by word of mouth from one generation to another.

Prophet – A person who speaks by divine inspiration; especially one through whom God reveals himself and expresses his will.

Protestantism – As the name suggests, people who object, especially to the teaching and form of the Church of Rome; hence the churches of the Reformation.

Qur'an – Literally 'reading' and is taken from the instruction which the Angel Jibril – Gabriel – gave to the Prophet Muhammad to read the word of God. The Qur'an is the holy book of the Muslim religion and it comprises of a series of messages or revelations from God given to the Prophet Muhammad over a period of 20 years during the sixth century CE.

Ramadan – The Islamic holy month during which the Prophet Muhammad received God's revelation.

Redemption – Meaning 'brought back' – redeemed from sin; forgiveness for past wrongs.

Reincarnation – The rebirth of the soul into a new body.

Religion – A system of faith and worship.

Resurrection – The belief prevalent in the Western Prophetic Tradition that on the Day of Judgement, God will raise people from the dead, with different religions offer differing doctrines as to the actual form this resurrection will take. For example, Christian belief is firmly rooted in the resurrection of Jesus.

Retribution – Punishment inflicted for past wrongs.

Roman Catholicism – Belonging to the Church of Rome. The Roman church traditionally regards itself as founded by its first bishop Peter and successor to Jesus himself. It lays store by the authority of the Church's tradition and the infallibility of the Pope. It is the largest single Christian denomination in the world.

Salvation – Saving of the soul and deliverance from sin. In Christian terms, salvation brought about by the death and resurrection of Jesus.

Sanskrit – The language of the Aryan peoples and of the Hindu scriptures. It is an Indo-European language related to Latin, Greek and Persian.

Semitic – Member of any of the races descended from Shem (Hebrew Bible, Genesis 10:21) including the Hebrews, Aramaeans, Phoenicians, Arabs and Assyrians.

Shaman – In primal religions, a person believed to be capable of direct contact with the spirit world. Also known as a medicine man or witch-doctor.

Shi'a – Means 'party' and refers to the followers of Ali. Shi'a Muslims believe that Ali, (died 661) the Prophet's cousin, married to the Prophet's daughter Fatima, and their descendents, were the rightful leaders of the Muslim community.

Sikhism – Founded in the 15th century CE by Guru Nanak in the area of modern-day Pakistan and northwest India known as Punjab. At a time of tension between Hindus and Muslims, Guru Nanak believed such religious conflicts were harmful and gathered around him a small group of followers who, like him, were searching for an understanding of God uncluttered by ritual.

Sophists – Teachers and philosophers of Ancient Greece who lived during the 4th and 5th centuries. Amongst them Protagorus who believed that 'the human-being is the measure of all things' and that 'things are as one says they are and sees them as being'.

Sunni – From the 'Sunna' or 'tradition' of the Prophet Muhammad; the form of Islam followed by Muslims who believe that the Prophet did not designate an heir on his death in 632 CE but left the decision to the community.

Swinburne, Richard – Born 1934, British philosopher.

Talmud – Judaism's commentary and discussion on the Hebrew Bible completed about 500 CE.

Tetragrammation – Four Hebrew letters for the name of God that are never pronounced in the Jewish Tradition.

Transcendence – Existing apart from; not subject to the limitations of the material universe.

Transmigration – After death, the soul re-attaching itself to another living form.

Universal Religions – These include Judaism, Christianity, Islam and other Eastern religions, which appeared later than the Primal Religions. Universal religions usually have scriptures, and often see themselves as applying universally to all peoples.

Utilitarianism – A philosophy first propounded in the 18th and 19th centuries by Jeremy Bentham and John Stuart Mill. Its main tenets are to provide the greatest happiness to the greatest number of people and to produce the greatest amount of good over evil.

Upanishads – Part of the Sruti, or Shruti ('hearings') Hindu sacred writings. The 108 Upanishads (meaning 'sit down near your teacher') were recorded between 800 and 300 BCE. They are also known as the Vedanta ('end of the Vedas') as they used to be the third section of the Vedas.

Voltaire, Francois Marie Arouet de (1694–1778) – French writer, poet, playwright, philosopher and historian. After his trip to England, he wrote about the freedom of thought he had found in England and in particular, the rights of men of literature against the power of religious authority, the king and the nobles.

Western Prophetic Tradition – Emphasises that God reveals His will to human-beings through a prophet such as Moses in the Hebrew Bible and Muhammad in the Qur'an.

Yom Kippur – The most solemn day of the Jewish calendar. Also known as the Day of Atonement, it is a time for fasting and asking God for forgiveness.

Resources

The following list of key resources is ordered by chapter, to make it easy to dip in and out of relevant sections as you read through this book. Some websites will inevitably change as time goes by. In such circumstances, a search engine such as Google or Alta Vista may be useful.

Preface

'Youth Matters' – green paper for information re spiritual development in young people www.dfes. gov.uk/publications/youth

Consultation on spirituality in preparation for green paper www.nya.org.uk

Chapter 1: What's the real me?

Terry Waite www.bbc.co.uk/onthisday/hi/witness

Chapter 2: What am I for?

Nelson Mandela www.tiscali.co.uk/reference/encyclopaedia

Martin Luther King www.tiscali.co.uk/reference/encyclopaedia

Mahatma Gandhi's life and philosophy www.mkgandhi.org

Mahatma Gandhi's concept of satyagraha www.ppu.org.uk/learn/infodocs/people/gandhi

Mahatma Gandhi Institute for Non-Violence www.gandhiinstitute.org

Vaclav Havel www.brainyquote.com

Ideas for positive action
  www.makepovertyhistory.org
  www.btplc.com/listening
  www.nya.org.uk/global
  www.learningpartnerships.org.uk
  www.yearofthevolunteer.org
  www.wavemakers.org.uk
  www.makingmusictogether.blogspot.com
  www.russellcommission.org

Chapter 3: Am I really alone?

Ideas for making the most of staying at home www.youthinformation.com

Chapter 4: Why do bad things happen?

General information 11–25 year olds www.cliconline.co.uk

Supporting bereaved young people www.scre.ac.uk/bereavement

Sexual health information www.likeitis.org.uk

Relationships www.ruthinking.co.uk

Chapter 5: Is there a God?

Information on Greek mythology www.pantheon.org/encyclopaedia.mythica

Information on pre-historic ancient Greek gods www.tiscali.co.uk/reference/encyclopaedia

Further exploration of belief and non-belief in God

> www.religioustolerance.org
> www.channel4.com/canyoubelieveit
> www.bbc.co.uk/worldreligions
> www.multifaithnet.org

Chapter 6: What happens next?

Plato www.rep.routledge.com

Carl Jung's theory of the Collective Unconscious www.psychenet.uk.com

Chapter 7: What do I believe?

Personality psychology

> www.personalityresearch.org/bigfive/jack.html
> www.myersbrigs.com
> www.belbin.com

Freud's view on the effect of childhood experience on belief in God in adulthood www.bbc.co.uk/religion/atheism

Atheism www.bbc.co.uk/religion/atheism

Agnosticism and famous agnostics www.religioustolerance.org

Humanism

British Humanist Association, 1 Gower Street London WC1 6HD Tel. 0207079 3580 www.humanism.org.uk

Nicolaus Copernicus www.channel4.com/believeitornot

Hinduism www.bbc.co.uk/worldservice/hinduism

www.hinduism-today.com

Buddhism www.buddhanet.net

Founded in 1924 and based in London www.thebuddhistsociety.org

Sikhism www.bbc.co.uk/worldservice/sikhism

www.sikhs.org

Judaism www.bbc.co.uk/worldservice/judaism

www.mucjs.org/laski

www.virtualjerusalem.com

Christianity www.bbc.co.uk/worldservice/christianity

www.multifaith.org/christianity

Islam in Britain www.guardian.co.uk/islam

www.bbc.co.uk/worldservice/islam

Chapter 8: What about spirituality?

Information on the emerging Tibetan Buddhist nunnery at Tashi Jong in N. India www.tenzinpalmo.com

Scheme to promote cultural tolerance www.encompasstrust.org

References and Useful Books

Primary sources

The Bhagavad Gita. (Hindu sacred text). Penguin Classics, 2003.

The Concise Oxford Dictionary. The Clarendon Press, 1964.

The Guru Granth Sahib. Parts 1 and 2 (Sikh sacred text). Motilal Banarsidass, 1996.

The Living Bible. (Christian Bible). Kingsway, 1971.

The Pali Canon: An Anthology of Discourses from the Pali Canon. (Buddhist sacred text). Wisdom Publications, 2005.

The Pentateuch and Haftorahs. (Jewish Hebrew Bible). Soncino, 1981.

The Qur'an. (Muslim sacred text). Maktaba Dar-us-Salam, 1997.

Secondary sources

Angeles, P. (1992) *The Harper Collins Dictionary of Philosophy.* Harper Perennial.

Argyle, M. (1983) *The Psychology of Interpersonal Behaviour.* Pelican.

Barnes, P. (2002) *Leadership With Young People.* Lyme Regis: Russell House Publishing.

Barnes, P. and Sharp, B. (2004) *The RHP Companion to Outdoor Education.* Lyme Regis: Russell House Publishing.

Barnes, T. (1999) *The Kingfisher Book of Religions.* Kingfisher.

Bowker, J. (1997) *World Religions.* Dorling Kindersley.

Carvalho, R. (1990) Psycho-dynamic Therapy: The Jungian Approach. In Dyden, W. (Ed.) *Individual Therapy: A Handbook.* Milton Keynes: Open University Press.

Christian, C. (1999) Spirituality in the Context of Multi-Cultural Youth Work. *Youth and Policy.* Autumn, 65: 38–47.

Clifton, J. and Serdar, H. (2000) *Bully Off!* Lyme Regis: Russell House Publishing.

Coffin, M.C. (Ed.) (2001) *The Complete Poetry and Selected Prose of John Donne.* Modern Library Classics.

Cooper, G. (1998) *Outdoors With Young People.* Lyme Regis: Russell House Publishing.

Costa, P.T. and McCrae, R.R. (1980) Influence of Extraversion and Neuroticism on Subjective Well-Being. *Journal of Personality and Social Psychology.* 38.

Costa, P.T. and McCrae, R.R. (1984) Personality as a Lifelong Determinant of Well-being. In Malatesta, C. and Izard, C. (Eds.) *Affective Processes in Adult Development and Ageing.* Beverley Hills, CA: Sage.

Feuerverger, G. (2001) *Oasis of Dreams.* Routledge Falmer.

Fontana, D. (1992) *Psychology for Professional Groups.* Macmillan.

Freud, S. (1991) *New Introductory Lectures on Psychoanalysis.* Penguin.

Gangrade, K.D. (2001) *Religion and Peace: A Gandhian Perspective.* Gandhi Smriti and Darshan Samiti.

Gibran, K. (1994) *The Prophet.* Bracken.

Harrison-Barbet, A. (1990) *Mastering Philosophy.* Macmillan.

Hay, D. with Nye, R. (1998) *The Spirit of the Child.* Fount.

Ingram, G. and Harris, J. (2001) *Delivering Good Youth Work.* Lyme Regis: Russell House Publishing.

Isaacson, B. (1979) *Dictionary of the Jewish Religion.* Bantan Books.

Keenan, P. (2004) *Philosophy of Religion: The Problem of Evil.* Teachers' Class Notes, St. Dominic's 6th Form College, Harrow.

Knight, S. (1997) *NLP at Work.* Nicholas Brealey Publishing.

Langley, M. (1993) *World Religions.* Lion.

Larkin, P. (1985) Aubade. *Times Literary Supplement.*

Mandela, N. (2000) *Long Walk to Freedom.* Abacus.

Mansukhani, G. Singh (1982) *Introduction to Sikhism.* Hemkunt Press.

March, J. (2000) *Dictionary of Classical Mythology.* Cassell.

McCrae, R.R (1987) Somatic Complaints as a Function of Age and Neuroticism: A Longitudinal Analysis. *Journal of Behavioural Medicine.* I3: 245–57.

Morrison, M. (2001) *Clear Speech.* A & C Black.

Moser, P. and McKay, G. (Eds.) (2005) *Community Music.* Lyme Regis: Russell House Publishing.

Mountain, A. (2004) *The Space Between.* Lyme Regis: Russell House Publishing.

Nacif, A.P. (2005) A Sense of Self. *Young People Now.* 15 Nov.

National Youth Agency (2005) *Spirituality and Spiritual Development in Youth Work.* NYA.

National Youth Agency (1999) *Helping Young People Find Their Place.* NYA.

Nicoll, A. (1961) *World Drama From Aeschylus to Anouilh.* Harrap.

Osborne, R. (1992) *Philosophy for Beginners.* Writers and Readers Publishing, Inc.

Otto, R. (1958) *The Idea of the Holy.* Oxford University Press.

Quiller-Couch, A. (1946) *The Oxford Book of English Verse.* Oxford.

Reber, A.S. and Reber, E. (2001) *The Penguin Dictionary of Psychology.* Penguin Books.

Robertson, S. (2005) *Youth Clubs.* Lyme Regis: Russell House Publishing.

Scholem, G. (1995) *Major Trends in Jewish Mysticism.* Schocken Books.

Schulweis, H.M. (1995) *For Those Who Can't Believe.* Harper Perennial.

Smith, A. (1994) *Creative Outdoor Work with Young People.* Lyme Regis: Russell House Publishing.

Taylor, A.M. (2003) *Responding to Adolescents.* Lyme Regis: Russell House Publishing.

Thompson, D. (2001) *Madonna: Queen of the World.* John Blake Publishing.

Waite, T. (1993) *Taken on Trust.* Hodder and Stoughton.

Weddell, K. (2006) *Dealing with Conflict.* Sessions of York.

Wheal, A. (1999) *Adolescence.* Lyme Regis: Russell House Publishing.

Wheal, A. (2002) *The RHP Companion to Leaving Care.* Lyme Regis: Russell House Publishing.

Whiting, J.R.S. (1983) *Religions of Man.* Stanley Thornes Ltd.